PENGUIN BOOKS

THE ROAD TO SANTIAGO DE COMPOSTELA

Dr Michael Jacobs studied at the Courtauld Institute of Art, University of London, and was awarded a doctorate in 1982. He is now a full-time writer and his publications include *The Phaidon Companion to Art and Artists in the British Isles* (with Malcolm Warner); *The Good and Simple Life: Artists' Colonies in Europe and America; Provence;* and *Andalusía.* Current projects are Blue Guides to Barcelona and Czechoslovakia and a book on Madrid. He has lived for long periods in Spain and has led study tours there.

Other titles in the series:
CLASSICAL TURKEY
IMPERIAL CHINA
ISLAMIC SPAIN
MUGHAL INDIA

In preparation:
ANCIENT EGYPT
CHÂTEAUX OF THE LOIRE
MEDIEVAL TUSCANY AND UMBRIA

To Javier Landa, Annie Bennett, and Matilde Mateo Sevilla
'fellow pilgrims'

THE ROAD TO
SANTIAGO DE COMPOSTELA

MICHAEL JACOBS

PENGUIN BOOKS

PENGUIN BOOKS

Published by the Penguin Group
Penguin Books Ltd, 27 Wrights Lane, London W8 5TZ, England
Viking Penguin, a division of Penguin Books USA Inc.
375 Hudson Street, New York, New York 10014, USA
Penguin Books Australia Ltd, Ringwood, Victoria, Australia
Penguin Books Canada Ltd, 2801 John Street, Markham, Ontario, Canada L3R 1B4
Penguin Books (NZ) Ltd, 182–190 Wairau Road, Auckland 10, New Zealand

Penguin Books Ltd, Registered Offices: Harmondsworth, Middlesex, England

Designed and produced by Johnson Editions Ltd
15 Grafton Square, London SW4 0DQ

First published in Great Britain by Viking 1991
Published in Penguin Books 1992
10 9 8 7 6 5 4 3 2 1

Series conceived by Georgina Harding
Editor: Louisa McDonnell
Series design: Clare Finlaison
Design: Wendy Bann
Maps and plans: David Woodroffe
Picture research: Emma Milne
Index: Hilary Bird

Typesetting: DP Photosetting, Aylesbury, Bucks
Origination: Fotographics, London-Hong Kong
Printed in Italy by Rotolito Lombarda Spa, Milan

CONTENTS

PREFACE

The reasons for travelling to Santiago de Compostela have always been many and varied, and range today from the purely spiritual to the sporting. For the increasing number of travellers who follow the pilgrims' way out of an interest in Spanish culture, there has been up to now no guide-book dealing specifically with the architecture of the route. Furthermore the innumerable specialist accounts devoted to the cultural history of the Santiago pilgrimage have concentrated largely on the early medieval period, ignoring the fact that the pilgrimage has been a near continuous activity from the ninth century right up to the present day. In describing, without chronological bias, the main monuments that line the pilgrims' way from the Pyrenees to Santiago, I have aimed to provide a brief introduction to Spanish architecture as a whole, a subject which in itself has been remarkably neglected.

The most convenient way of visiting the places described in this book is by your own car, though there are now a growing number of travel companies that organize cultural tours that take in most of the best known monuments along the route; a leisurely tour by car or coach can be done in about eight to ten days. However, to be considered a *bona fide* pilgrim, and to be presented in Santiago with your pilgrim's certificate or *Compostellana*, you are obliged either to walk, cycle or go on horseback. Before setting off you should acquire a 'pilgrim's passport', which is essential both for receiving your certificate and for staying at the many pilgrims' refuges along the way; these refuges, at their most basic, offer a mattress on the floor, though some also have showers and cooking facilities. Once you have obtained your certificate you are supposedly entitled to three days of food at the luxury Hostal de Los Reyes Católicos in Santiago; it should be added, however, that much depends on how many pilgrims are in town, and that in any case you are forced to eat an uninspired set menu at an impractically early hour, and sealed off like a leper from the hotel guests.

(Opposite) The west portal of San Salvador de Vilar de Donas, Galicia.

vii

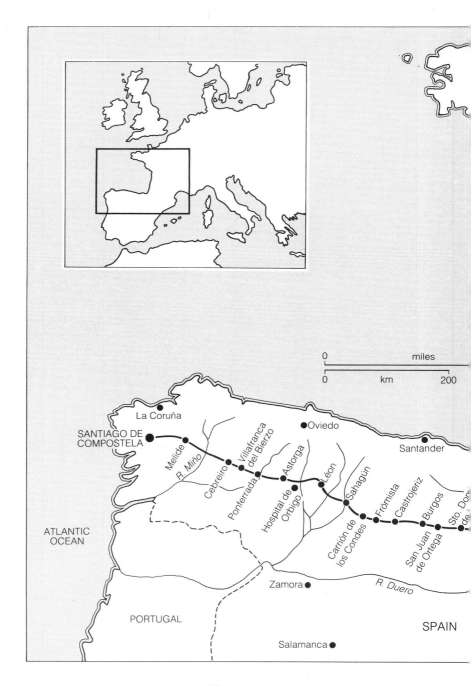

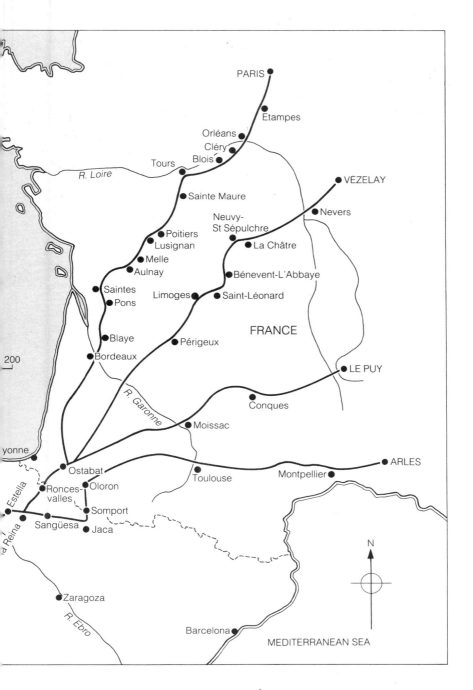

Should you decide to go as a pilgrim to Santiago, you are likely to receive much more hospitality generally if you avoid the crowded months of July and August. The walk to Santiago from the Pyrenees (a distance of around 400 km/250 miles) takes between four and five weeks, averaging an optimum 25 km (15 miles) a day. However, unless you are doing the pilgrimage as a penance or as a sporting challenge, there seems little point in walking the whole length of the route. Long and dangerous stretches of main road, and the dreary approaches to large towns such as Burgos and León are best done by public transport. Bus services are frequent from the Pyrenees up to Burgos, and though less good thereafter, you can always make use of the cheap local taxis, which are quite accustomed to picking up exhausted pilgrims. To be awarded your *Compostellana*, you need only to have walked 100 km (60 miles), and thus the occasional resort to public transport is quite acceptable. If your time is limited, the most beautiful and exciting stretches are to be found between Astorga and Santiago, where you will usually find yourself far from the main roads, often on remote footpaths affording spectacular views.

I make no apologies for linking my discussion of the architecture of the pilgrims' way with descriptions of the actual route. Following the road to Santiago makes you aware more than ever of how architecture should not be seen in a stylistic void, but should be considered not only in its historical and social contexts, but also in its geographical one. As you slowly make your way to Santiago, walking every evening in the direction of the setting sun, you will begin to see buildings in a different way, the humblest of monuments becoming transformed by the beauty of the landscape, by the exhilaration of arriving there after hours of arduous wandering, and by the sense of accomplishing another stage in a journey towards some ultimate goal.

INTRODUCTION

St James and the pilgrimage

The story of **St James** and of the pilgrimage in his honour brings together an unsavoury mixture of religious propaganda, political opportunism and commercial greed, but like all stories that have captured the imagination of millions has an element of undeniable mystery. Surely, for instance, it is not just coincidence that the saint's shrine is situated near a point in Europe which was known to the ancients as '*Finis Terrae*', and must once have inspired considerable awe. As with other Christian pilgrimages — such as that to the Virgin of the Rocío in the Guadalquivir esturary — it is quite possible that the Santiago one superseded some pagan cult, in this case one born of the impulse which drew worshippers to the edge of the known world.

The historical evidence for the apostle James ever having been to Spain is extremely flimsy, and the first mention that he went there dates suspiciously from as late as the eighth century. The story goes that St James, obeying Christ's instructions to spread the word of the Bible as widely as possible, decided to try his luck in Spain, but was only to be posthumously successful there. After failing to convert Spain to Christianity, he returned to the Holy Land, where he was beheaded in AD 44 and his body thrown to dogs. The remains were picked up by two of his disciples and taken by boat to Iria Flavia in Galicia. Numerous scholars have tried to supply a more rational explanation of how the relics of the apostle should have ended up in a remote corner of north-western Spain, the most plausible being that the relics were originally brought to an Egyptian monastery and then transfered around the sixth century to Galicia by Coptic monks on their way to Ireland.

The relics, whether genuine or not, were not to be 'discovered' until 814, the man responsible being one Bishop Theodomir, who had been guided there, like the Magi to Bethlehem, by a star. Stars play an important role in the

1

The Disembarcation of the body of Santiago by The Master of Astorga (Lázaro Galdiano Museum, Madrid).

Santiago story, for it was a constellation which was also supposed to have pointed Charlemagne in the direction of the saint's tomb; the pilgrims' route is often referred to as the 'Milky Way', and it has traditionally been thought that the name 'Compostela' is a derivative of the Latin *'campus stellae'* or 'field of stars'. Sadly, the latter theory was undermined after the Second World War, when excavations under Santiago cathedral revealed an ancient burial site or *compostum*, a word from which is also derived our rather unpoetic term, 'compost heap'. These excavations did at least corroborate one aspect of the St James story — that Bishop Theodomir did exist, for his tomb was found, thus confounding those cynics who believed that he too was a figment of the imagination.

With the development of the St James cult after the ninth century, the dividing line between fact and fiction became increasingly blurred, with the church authorities even exploiting the confusion which arose between James the apostle and James the Lesser. The eighth-century exploits of **Charlemagne**, as romanticized in the 11th-century *Song of Roland*, contributed their own fanciful appeal to the St James story; contrary to popular belief, the Holy Roman Emperor never went as far as Galicia, but his and Roland's putative deeds on the pilgrims' route, such as falling down on his knees to pray towards Santiago, or Roland's splitting of a giant boulder at Roncesvalles, endowed Jacobean legend with a gloss of chivalric romance. A rather less attractive development of the St James story was the invention in the ninth century of Santiago Matamoros, or St James the Moor-Slayer. In a battle supposedly between Ramiro I and the Moors in 844 near Clavijo (no such battle is in fact known to have taken place), St James miraculously appeared on a horse and led the Christians to victory. In gratitude to the saint, Ramiro subsequently decreed that all people of Spain should make an annual offering in perpetuity to the saint's church at Santiago de Compostela: this tax, known as the *Voto de Santiago*, was to be imposed right up to the 19th century. The chauvinistic notion of St James as a bloodthirsty killer of Moors was not a universally popular one, and the authenticity of the document proposing the tax to him was to be heavily disputed over the centuries. However, the growing number of critics of the saint, though supported by the forces of Reason, were never able to

St James the Moor-Slayer — detail of frontispiece of Hostal de San Marcos, Leon.

dispel once and for all the very stories on which one of the most important of all pilgrimages was based.

Pilgrims probably first began visiting the saint's tomb at Santiago shortly after 814, but the earliest to be documented was the Bishop of Le Puy, who came here in 951. Over 45 years later Islamic forces from southern Spain, led by Almanzor, devastated Santiago and its cathedral. The pilgrimage, though temporarily suspended, was subsequently renewed with ever increasing fervour, and in the course of the 11th century was used by the church as a forceful instrument of propaganda in the so-called Christian 'Reconquest' of Spain. The great powers of the day recognized also the political and commercial gains of the pilgrimage. The majority of the pilgrims were at first from France, and the main route which they followed through Spain (soon to be known as the *Camino Francés* or French Way), helped to unite France and the then separate kingdoms of Christian Spain, and served too as one of the most important commercial thoroughfares of Europe.

A pioneering Spanish promoter of the route in the early 11th century was **Sancho the Great** of Navarre, while at the end of the century a vital role in supporting it was played by **Alfonso VI** of Castille and **Sancho Ramírez**, king of Aragón and Navarre. The last two monarchs encouraged French settlers to come to Spain, and as a result considerable French communities grew up in such places along the route as Sangüesa, Pamplona, Estella, and Villafranca del Bierzo. Alfonso VI, one of the most Francophile of Spain's kings, also had a significant influence on the route through commissioning the construction of bridges and the improvement of road surfaces, tasks which were largely carried out by two saintly engineers, **St Dominic** and the latter's pupil, **St John of Ortega**. By the beginning of the following century, another major propagandist of the pilgrimage had emerged in the towering figure of **Diego Gelmírez**, first Archbishop of Santiago, and a man whose intellect, energy and ambition did much to consolidate the international reputation of his town. At the same time the French monastery of **Cluny** dramatically extended its revolutionary influence through the setting up along the route of numerous sister institutions and hostels caring for pilgrims, the largest being that of Sahagún. Other monastic orders such as the Cistercians and Antonines followed suit, and the 12th century saw also the establishment in Spain of the Templars, the Hospitallers, and the Knights of Santiago, militant church orders who took responsibility for the defence of pilgrims on the ever more congested road to Santiago.

The monastery of Cluny was responsible for the commissioning in the early 12th century of the manuscript known as the *Codex Calixtinus*, a collection of texts relating to St James and his worship. Book V of this work comprises what is generally thought of as the first guide-book in history. Its author, usually identified with the Poitou priest called **Aymeric Picaud**, gives a delightfully opinionated account of the peoples, places and sites to be seen on the way to Santiago. The book is full of practical hints, for instance advice to pilgrims on what water they should or should not drink, and warnings to be wary of inn-keepers, who are accused of over-charging and other illicit practices. Picaud divided the *Camino Francés* into 13 clearly defined stages, and also identified the four main routes through France which linked up with it: one of these went through Arles and Toulouse, another began at the Burgundian shrine of Vézelay, a third crossed the Auvergne, and a final one joined together the towns of Orleans, Tours and Bordeaux, with a possible extension to the north to take in Paris (see map on pages viii and ix).

In its earlier days the pilgrimage had largely appealed to an aristocratic milieu, but by Picaud's time it had come to attract every social class. It was also becoming much more interna-

K.J. Conant's reconstruction of the Abbey of Cluny, Burgundy; bird's-eye view from the south-east as in 1157.

5

Medieval cross
marking the pilgrims'
way near the village
of Azofra in the Rioja.

tional in its scope than Picaud's guide suggested, and had started to draw people from well beyond the confines of France. Travellers from as far afield as Holland, Germany, Scandinavia and Italy would converge on to the four routes through France, and, furthermore, there were many alternative routes to the *Camino Francés*, albeit none as well trodden: thus there were Portuguese and Catalan routes, and, for English pilgrims, a maritime route which landed you either at the Galician port of La Coruña or else forced you to follow a road along Spain's wild and mountainous northern coast.

Most of the pilgrims, no matter where they came from, could expect a journey away from home of at least four months; many were gone several years, and many never returned at all. Cheered off by their townspeople or fellow villagers, they tended to travel in large groups of up to 30, but this security measure guaranteed only partial protection from the countless bandits who lay in wait for them along the route; they faced in addition the physical rigours of the journey, and the occasional treachery of their companions, who sometimes stole and even committed murder. Many hours of continual prayer awaited them on their arrival at Santiago, where they would be awarded their precious *Compostellana*, a document which was much more than a mere record of their great journey; it was also a plenary indulgence, offering remission from purgatory. It had in addition the practical value of granting trading rights along the *Camino Francés*, a fact which led to its being frequently sold on the black market. Another essential acquisition at Santiago was a scallop shell. The scallop remains to this day one of the gastronomic delights of Galicia, though why its shell — the ancient symbol of Venus and the vagina — should have been made into the emblem of the pilgrimage is not known. The shells that the pilgrims obtained were at first natural ones, though by the 12th century a thriving trade in jade and metal badges had resulted in scenes of frenzied commercial activity outside the cathedral doors at Santiago.

The religious, political and commercial advantages of promoting the pilgrimage might be obvious, but what did the majority of pilgrims have to gain by making the journey? The prospect of losing time in purgatory was of course an important motive, though there were numerous others, the most fundamental of all being connected with the obsessive medieval cult of relics. The cult had developed around the fourth century AD, and been criticized from the very start, many feeling it to reflect an entirely pagan mentality. Most worshippers, however, were convinced that relics of saints had some of the qualities of the saints in life, and helped to assuage the very real fear of evil which existed in the Middle Ages. Relics were collected with the same fervour which in later centuries would be reserved for the acquisition of works of art, and drew vast crowds of admirers, especially as they tended to be displayed in shrines of astonishing sumptuousness. The medieval cult of relics had in many ways much in common with the present-day approach to sightseeing, in which pleasure is combined with a belief in the uplifting qualities of art and architecture, and with an almost ritualistic desire to 'tick off' a given series of famous sights. One of the most detailed sections in Picaud's guide is devoted to the numerous shrines — such as at Tours, Limoges, Conques and Toulouse — that had grown up along the route to Santiago, and that provided pilgrims with the necessary spiritual distractions to sustain them on their journey.

The reliquary of Sainte Foy, Conques, south-west France.

The journey to Santiago was undoubtedly regarded by many as a process of spiritual cleansing, and the ritual of pilgrims bathing just before reaching Santiago, was filled with symbolical meaning. The very hardships and dangers of the journey were an essential part of the process, for pilgrims could feel that they were taking part in a secular crusade, or even identify with the sufferings of Christ. Yet it must also be said that the sense of adventure was in itself a sufficient inducement for many people to undertake the pilgrimage. One such adventurer was the 15th-century English pilgrim Andrew Boorde, whose cynicism about the authenticity of St James' relics did not prevent him from doing the journey to Santiago twice, and who died, significantly, in a Fleet Street prison, accused of living with three women simultaneously. There were several complaints that the motives of many of the pilgrims were scarcely religious, but stemmed instead from 'curiosity to see new places, to experience new things, impatience of the servant with his master, or children with their parents, or wives with their husbands'. Other critics spoke disdainfully of those who ate and drank their way to Santiago, or regretted the presence of women pilgrims, who were held responsible for all the promiscuity which apparently existed on the Santiago route. Quite clearly the pilgrimage attracted too the underbelly of society — the professional beggars, the black-marketeers, ruthless tradesmen, and those evading tax or persecution from criminal activities.

There exists a rather romantic belief that in the early Middle Ages the Santiago pilgrimage was at its most spiritual, and that in later years it took on a more decadent character. The fact remains, however, that virtually all the surviving pilgrim accounts date from the late 15th century onwards and that much of what is written about the pilgrimage in its early days is based upon speculation. In any case the pilgrimage seems to have gained in importance as the Middle Ages wore on, certainly in terms of the numbers of pilgrims involved. After the defeat of the Moorish Kingdom of Granada in 1492, more people than ever appear to have made the journey to Santiago. The Reformation and the strictures of preachers such as Erasmus might have led to a greatly diminished presence from northern countries, but from elsewhere in Europe many pilgrims continued to visit the shrine throughout the 16th, 17th and 18th centuries, when some of the finest monuments along the *Camino Francés* were created. Only in the 19th century did the number of pilgrims to Santiago decline in an alarming way, but even so, this was only to be a short-lived phenomenon. Excavations in Santiago cathedral in 1879 located the skull of St James, the authenticity of which was proved — at least in the eyes of the church authorities — by the existence in Pistoia cathedral of a fragment of the apostle's skull which matched exactly a missing piece in the Santiago one. The popularity of the pilgrimage was renewed, and has continued to increase in recent years, fuelled perhaps by a slightly bogus medieval nostalgia. The anachronistic aspects of the present-day pilgrim were highlighted in Luis Buñuel's delightfully satirical film, *The Milky Way*.

Whatever your motives in travelling to Santiago, it is undeniable that the journey to get there from the Pyrenees will give you a wonderful insight into the variety of the landscapes, food and peoples of northern Spain, and provide too a remarkably full introduction to Spanish architecture.

A 16th-century woodcut of German pilgrims on the road to Santiago.

The architecture of the *Camino Francés*

In considering the buildings that lie along the pilgrims' way, the fascinating examples of Spain's diverse folk architecture should not be ignored: especially interesting are the *pallozas* at the Galician hamlet of Cebreiro, oval-shaped buildings that probably give a good idea of what popular dwellings were like in Spain before the coming of the Romans in the third century BC. Of Roman architecture, there is unfortunately little to be seen in the vicinity of the pilgrims' way, and the same holds true of the architecture of their successors, the Visigoths, who first popularized the use of the horseshoe arch in Spain. This form was later adopted by the **Moors**, who entered the country after AD 711, and were to exercise a most profound influence on the whole history of Spanish architecture. Though the north of Spain has no Moorish building as celebrated as those in the south, you will see here several fine examples of so-called **Mozarabic** architecture — the work of Christians who had been brought up in a Moorish environment. The largest Mozarabic building in Spain is the isolated church of San Miguel de Escalada near León, which was constructed in the ninth century by Christians fleeing from Córdoba, and, with its forest of columns, is reminiscent of the Great Mosque at Córdoba. Borrowings from Moorish architecture are also to be found in Spanish architecture of the **Romanesque** period, for instance in the vaulting of the Templar chapel at Torres del Río, or in the cusped arching in churches such as San Isidoro in León and San Pablo at Estella.

Interior of San Miguel de Escalada, near León.

The presence too of Moorish motifs in some of the Romanesque buildings along the pilgrims' route through France (most notably in the area around Poitiers) draws attention to the way in which the Santiago pilgrimage was of vital importance in the spread of artistic and architectural ideas from one country to the other. Unfortunately the whole issue of a 'pilgrimage style' is clouded by intense chauvinism, Spanish and French historians all bitterly arguing about the originality of their respective country's achievements. What is certain is that the masons, sculptors and architects who worked along the pilgrims' routes led very itinerant lives, as is revealed, for instance, in the way in which a particular hand can be identified in the sculptures of a number of churches

The Romanesque church of San Martín at Frómista.

situated sometimes hundreds of miles apart. Moreover the five main churches associated with the Santiago pilgrimage — the cathedral at Santiago itself, St Martin at Tours, Saint-Martial at Limoges, Sainte-Foy at Conques, and Saint-Sernin at Toulouse — are characterized by similar ground-plans and elevations. All have long naves with arches and triforium galleries, wide transepts, and apses with radiating chapels. These were buildings of monumental proportions intended to accommodate as many pilgrims as possible with the minimal interruption to the liturgical functions.

Whereas there is a strong case in favour of mutual influences between Spain and France during the Romanesque period, the dominant influence of France during the **Gothic** period is unquestionable. The Cistercians brought from France into Spain the first tentative Gothic forms, and the architects of Spain's great Gothic cathedrals such as those at León and Burgos were wholly familiar with contemporary French buildings such as the cathedrals of Chartres, Rheims and Bourges. None the less there remains something unmistakeably Spanish about a building such as Burgos cathedral, which, even before being encrusted with ornament from the

Part of Burgos cathedral.

late 15th century onwards, lacked the uncluttered elegance and soaring proportions of a French Gothic cathedral, having instead a characteristically Spanish heaviness. Peculiarly Spanish too is the way in which this country's cathedrals have choirs placed right across the nave, thus impeding a clear view down to the chancel, and creating an often confusing effect which the rationally-minded French architects would have abhorred. It must also be borne in mind that throughout the medieval period Moorish craftsmen who had remained in Christian Spain — the so-called *Mudéjars*, an Arabic word meaning both 'to stay behind' and 'to be tamed' — were active in the embellishment and even the construction of many Spanish buildings. They revelled in delicate brickwork patterned with elaborate blind arcading; and to many a Romanesque or Gothic structure they added an exotic, oriental touch through their complex *artesonado* or wooden ceilings, imitative of leatherwork.

The full originality of Spanish architecture becomes especially apparent after the late 15th century, under the influence at first of a generation of architects and sculptors who though mainly of north European descent came to be naturalized Spaniards and thoroughly immersed in Spanish ways. Figures such as Simón de Colonia, Enrique de Egas, and Gil and Diego de Siloe were active, significantly, both as sculptors and architects. As with most of the finest Spanish architects of later generations, their approach to architecture was thoroughly sculptural and unintellectual, with a heavy reliance on exuberant ornamentation. The term **plateresque**, which is derived from the Spanish word for silversmith (*platero*), has come to be used to describe much Spanish architecture of the late 15th and early 16th centuries. Inspired possibly by the surface complexities of the *Mudéjar* craftsmen, the plateresque architects went in for ornamental effects of exceptional intricacy, and exploited to the full the decorative possibilities of lettering; they loved to crown their buildings with elaborate balustrades bristling with finials, and made extensive use of large-scale heraldic motifs, relishing in particular naturalistic forms such as scallop shells. The work of the 16th-century architects is often distinguished from that of earlier ones by being termed 'classical' rather than 'Gothic' plateresque, but though they favoured classical ornamental motifs instead of the more

The plateresque frontispiece of the Hostel de los Reyes Católicos, Santiago de Compostela.

playful Gothic types, their approach to architecture would have horrified their Italian Renaissance contemporaries. A typically Spanish top-heaviness was created by the placing of a gallery on the top rather than on the ground-floor of a building, and the architects of this period continued also to favour so-called 'retable façades', in which ornament was piled high in clearly differentiated layers, as in the medieval retables that rise up to the ceiling in many a Spanish church.

One of the paradoxes of Spanish architecture is the conflict between excessive ornamentation and uncompromising austerity: thus in the magnificent façade of the Hostal de los Reyes Católicos in Santiago a plateresque frontispiece is flanked by virtually undecorated masonry. In the late 16th century, under the influence of Juan de Herrera, Spanish architecture achieved a severity unprecedented elsewhere in Europe, with decoration abandoned almost completely, and materials limited to slate and granite. Elements of the Herrera style lingered on in Spanish architecture of the 17th and 18th centuries, but often alongside an exuberant ornamental vocabulary which makes that of the plateresque period seem quite tame in comparison; such ornamentation is named **Churrigueresque** in reference to the Churrigueras, an architectural dynasty from Salamanca who were in fact the least Churrigueresque of Spain's baroque architects. In Spanish buildings of this period elaborate ornamentation is usually applied to relatively simple structures, and rarely do you find the dynamic ground plans and elevations that are such a feature of the Italian or Central European baroque. Most of the finest 17th- and 18th- century buildings to be seen in northern Spain are concentrated in Santiago de Compostela, which, contrary to many people's expectations, is a superficially baroque town, indeed one of the finest in Europe. Few other baroque façades can compare in decorative inventiveness with **Casas y Nóvoa's** for Santiago cathedral, a pinnacled and fantastical assemblage of every conceivable ornament, and an appropriately spectacular *finale* for the followers of the pilgrims' road.

The extraordinary achievements of the Spanish baroque are not widely appreciated, but then neither were most other aspects of Spanish architecture until comparatively recently. The travellers who poured into Spain in the wake of the romantic 'discovery' of the country in the late 18th century were primarily interested in the Moorish monuments, and often dismissed the rest either as bizarre provincial works or else reflections of religious fanaticism. These travellers headed to the Moorish south, and relatively few spent long periods in the north; very few took any interest in the pilgrims' way. One of the exceptions was **Richard Ford**, whose remarkable *Handbook for Spain* of 1845 contained descriptions of such neglected works of the time as the Romanesque Pórtico de la Gloria at Santiago cathedral. Interest in Spain's medieval architecture was awakened further by the English Gothic architect **George Edmund Street**, who in 1865 published the pioneering *Gothic Architecture in Spain.* In this work Street confessed that his journey to Santiago had been 'quite an experiment' and that 'he had been able to learn nothing whatever about the cathedral before going there'. The discovery, behind Casas y Nóvoa's façade, of a Romanesque cathedral of 'extreme magnificence and interest' was a revelation to him, as was his first sight of the Pórtico de la Gloria, which he hailed as 'one of the greatest glories of Christian art'; his enthusiasm for the latter was endorsed shortly afterwards by a plaster cast being made of it for the cast gallery at London's Victoria and Albert Museum. Street's failings, however, were that his constant points of comparison were the great works of French medieval architecture, and that he frequently found Spanish buildings to fall short of this ideal. Generally he disliked the eccentricities of Spanish architecture, and he had little time for the plateresque, let alone for the baroque. The French bias of Gothicists such as Street, and the strictly classical tastes of others, impeded a serious discussion of the plateresque until early this century. As for the Spanish baroque, it has only been the subject of scholarly research in recent years, and even so it is rarely mentioned in the context of the architecture of the pilgrims' way. Though Santiago is a heavily baroque town, and though most of the churches that line the road to it belong to many periods, there remains a belief that the Romanesque style was the style most expressive of the ideals of the Santiago pilgrimage. For many people the simplicity of the Romanesque reflects a pure innocent devotion, which they romantically believe, against all historical evidence, to have been the state in which most pilgrims once set out on their long journey to Santiago.

The frontispiece from G. E. Street's *Some Account of Gothic Architecture in Spain,* London, 1865.

ARAGÓN
SOMPORT TO EUNATE

The Pyrenees represent one of the major stages in the journey to Santiago. They mark not only the Spanish frontier, but also — to those coming from northern Europe — the point where the pilgrims' route turns definitively to the west. The goal of the pilgrimage seems closer, and yet to medieval travellers these mountains must also have presented their greatest challenge so far. Added to the rigours of the climb were the considerable dangers provided by snow and wolves, and the hostility of a local population wary of the countless foreigners who, from prehistoric times, have penetrated into Spain by way of the two major passes across the Pyrenees. The northernmost of these, Valcarlos, was used by those pilgrims who had travelled along the routes from Paris, Le Puy and Vézelay. The other, known to the Romans as *Summus Portus* (Somport) was taken by those coming from Arles and Italy. This last is the steeper, higher and more dramatic of the two crossings, and takes you at the top into a landscape of gaunt granite peaks crowned with snow for much of the year. For the sick and tired pilgrims of the Middle Ages, this bleak and lonely pass had at least the consoling presence of what was at that time one of the most important hospitals in Europe, Santa Cristina. However, in the course of religious wars with Navarre in the 14th century, the hospital declined and was eventually abandoned. The number of pilgrims coming to Spain over the Somport Pass dwindled almost to nothing, and, even today far fewer pilgrims choose this route.

(Opposite) The nave of Jaca cathedral.

The Somport route, which joins up with the northern one at the Navarre town of Puente la Reina, is known in Spain as the *Camino Aragonés*. Crossing for 90 km (55 miles) the narrow north-western corner of Aragón, it at first follows the mountain river which gave this large region its name. Aragón, described by the 19th-century writer Richard Ford as a 'disagreeable region' filled with a 'disagreeable people', is

THE CAMINO ARAGONÉS

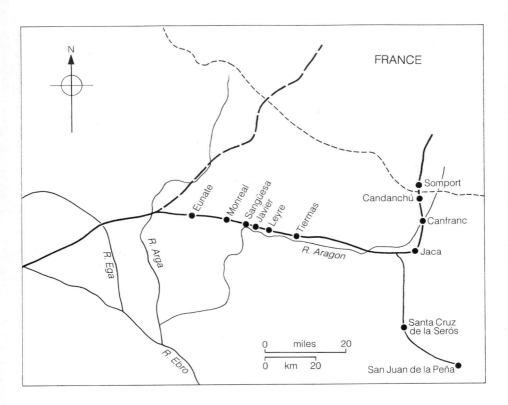

N

FRANCE

Eunate
Monreal
Sangüesa
Javier
Leyre
Tiermas

Somport
Candanchú
Canfranc

Candanchú

Canfranc

Jaca

R. Ega
R. Arga
R. Aragon
R. Ebro

Santa Cruz
de la Serós

0   miles   20

0   km   20

San Juan de la Peña

The pilgrims' way from Somport to Eunate.

traditionally known for the obstinacy and hot-headedness of its inhabitants. These latter qualities, admitted Ford, also made these people brave and excellent fighters, and in fact it is this tiny corner of Aragón crossed by the pilgrims' way which is supposed to have been the last Spanish district to have given in to the Moors after 715 and the first one to have expelled them. This very same area formed the original nucleus of the Kingdom of Aragón, which was not created until 1035, a good 200 years after the Moors' expulsion. Its founder, Ramiro I Sánchez, turned Jaca into both its capital and sole bishopric. But it was under his son and successor, Sancho Ramírez (1063–94) that this small mountain kingdom developed into a major economic, political and cultural force. Sancho Ramírez established at Jaca a *Fuero* or municipal charter which was to serve as a model for many others throughout Spain. The cities of Aragón were granted a Parliament as well as numerous civic liberties that they were to guard jealously well after the Unification of Castile and Aragón in 1469. In addition Aragón experienced under Sancho Ramírez a major building boom, and it was thanks to him that today's traveller along the *Camino Aragonés* will pass by some of the most important monuments in the early history of the Spanish Romanesque.

From the time of Sancho Ramírez, Aragón rapidly expanded in size. Although the union between Aragón and Navarre lasted only between 1076 and 1134, the kingdom considerably extended its territory to the south as more and more land was captured from the Moors. Finally, in 1137, the marriage between the Infanta Petronila with Count Ramón Berenguer IV led to the annexation of Aragón with Catalonia. As Aragón continued to grow, however, Jaca's own importance diminished, and indeed in 1118 it had been replaced as capital of the kingdom by the southern town of Zaragoza. Significantly, there are few post-Romanesque monuments of any importance along the *Camino Aragonés*, and, as you leave the Pyrenees at Jaca and descend into the vast valley which extends towards Navarre, you will go through a largely deserted countryside with many semi-abandoned villages.

The first stretch of the *Camino Aragonés*, according to Picaud's guide, led from the Gascon village of Borce to the district capital of Jaca. The route known to Picaud is almost exactly that of the modern road, and the pilgrim on foot has to walk mainly on asphalt all the way from Borce to Puente la Reina.

JACA

Jaca, the main town on the *Camino Aragonés*, was an ancient frontier fortress built by the Romans in 195 BC, and taken by the Moors in *c.* 716. After the Moors were ousted in *c.* 810, the fortress became the principal base for the Christian recapture of Aragón. Its heyday was the 11th century, and it became capital of the newly created kingdom of Aragón in 1035, and then seat of the Aragonese bishopric in 1042. Its situation on the pilgrims' way, combined with strong trading links with France, led to the rapid expansion of the town during this period. By the end of the 11th century the town was divided into two distinct areas – the walled 'Burgo San Nicolas', and, on the outer side of the walls, the 'Burgo Novo'.

The latter district was demolished in 1596 to make way for the large citadel on the western side of town; the walls were pulled down as late as 1917, their site being clearly marked by a semi-circular promenade commanding an extensive panorama. The town has grown in recent years into a very popular winter and summer resort, and there has been much uninspired modern development. None the less Jaca remains a relatively small place, and there is a tiny medieval district crossed by narrow, dark streets of considerable character.

At the heart of medieval Jaca is the 11th-century **Cathedral,** the oldest surviving in Spain, and begun, it is thought, at some time between 1035 and 1054; its construction coincides with the town's elevation into the capital of a kingdom. The cathedral's squat, heavily-built and much-altered exterior, tightly hemmed in by the surrounding buildings, is not immediately impressive, though a closer look reveals some rich Romanesque carvings belying the overall severity. The earliest parts of the building are considered to be the apse and west end, the latter dominated by a wide bell-tower supporting eight bells. The west portal, protected by a spacious narthex which was originally open at the sides, has a strong paleo-Christian character, evident in the Roman-inspired capitals and in the iconography of the tympanum, which comprises lions flanking a rosette symbolizing the Trinity. Of the three apses, only the right-hand one retains its original exterior featuring fantastical carvings of animals and elaborate vegetal motifs. The most attractive aspect of the cathedral's exterior is unquestionably its southern side, which faces a picturesque arcade where markets have been held since medieval times. The southern portal was remodelled in the 16th century but many of the original Romanesque capitals were retained, including a highly sophisticated carving of the Sacrifice of Isaac. In front of this portal is a small 16th-century loggia incorporating capitals taken from various parts of the original building, most notably from the destroyed cloister and upper choir; especially fine are the capitals of David and Saint Sixtus, the latter being a unique Romanesque representation of this Athenian pope.

Powerful Romanesque carvings adorn the massive capitals that surround the wide and atmospherically dark interior. Despite fanciful later additions, this interior retains an essentially 11th-century character; it has a most solemn and elegant nave, arranged in double bays, and with round columns alternating with grouped piers. The walls above the nave arcade are plain, and seem once to have supported a wooden roof, though this was replaced in the 16th century by elaborate star-vaulting, as were the roofs of the aisles. The barrel-vaulting of the 'included transepts' (transepts that do not project further than the aisles) is of the original Romanesque structure, and so too is the extraordinary crossing dome. This rests on an octagonal dome formed by trumpet squinches, and has four intersecting ribs projecting from each side of the octagon, just as in Moorish constructions. The main apse was destroyed in the late 18th century to make way for a long chancel decorated with lifeless frescoes; in 1918 the cathedral choir was transferred here. The other chapels and furnishings are mainly of the 16th century, the chapel of San Miguel (off the south transept) having on the outside extensive plateresque ornamentation by one Giovanni Moreto. The Romanesque cloister off the north side of the cathedral was destroyed at the same time as the main apse, and replaced by a dull, neoclassical version. A visit here is made worthwhile, however, by the fascinating Diocesan Museum which is arranged around the cloister. In the museum there has been assembled a remarkable series of Romanesque and Gothic frescoes from various churches in the vicinity, the whole forming the largest collection of Spanish medieval wall paintings outside the Museo de Arte de Catalonia in Barcelona.

SANTA CRUZ DE LA SERÓS

After leaving Jaca the pilgrims' way follows for over 97 km (60 miles) the main road to Pamplona, the N 240. A short and almost obligatory deviation from the route (and one made by most of the medieval pilgrims) is to turn south 10 km (6 miles) west of Jaca and take the side road marked San Juan de la Peña. The first place which you come to, the pretty village of Santa Cruz de la Serós, stands in a wooded fold of the wild Sierra de la Peña. It has two Romanesque churches, both of which were once attached to monastic institutions. The first one which you pass is **San Caprasio**, a toy-like structure which has been fully restored in recent years. The tower with paired openings is of the late 12th century, but the rest of this simple building belongs to a slightly earlier period; the walls of the

The former convent church of Santa María, Santa Cruz de la Serós, seen from the road leading up to the monastery of San Juan de la Peña.

nave and apse are decorated with blind arcading, while inside are Lombard bands. Whereas San Caprasio once formed part of a small monastery, the next church **Santa María**, belonged to the most important convent in Aragón. Founded in 995 by Count Sancho Garcés and his wife Doña Urracca, it was restored in the 11th century by her niece Doña Sancha; the widowed Doña Sancha retired here with her two sisters Teresa and Urraca. The surviving church is one of the most impressive Romanesque structures in Aragón, and its exterior makes a much more immediate impact than that of Jaca cathedral. This tri-apsidal structure in the form of a stubby cross is dominated by a tall transeptal tower elegantly decorated in its upper level by three superimposed paired openings, the whole blending in perfectly with the mountainous backdrop behind. The west portal echoes that of Jaca cathedral, with a tympanum comprising a rosette flanked by lions. The interior, at present being stripped of later accretions, has a high altar of 1495 and a holy water stoup formed of inverted capitals taken from the destroyed Romanesque cloister. But the highpoint of a visit here is the climb up into the tower, off which is a hidden vaulted chapel where the nuns would hide in the course of Saracenic invasions.

SAN JUAN DE LA PEÑA

From Santa Cruz de la Serós, the road slowly winds its way up the Sierra de la Peña to the former monastery of San Juan, a spectacular drive up a mountain streaked with strange reddish-ochre rock formations protruding out of a dense covering of southern pines. At the final bend in the road, a breath-takingly extensive panorama of the distant snow-capped Pyrenees is revealed. The Irish writer, Walter Starkie, making this journey in the 1920s, thought that the setting of the monastery would be ideal for a production of Wagner's *Parsifal*.

The monastery itself is completely hidden, and only comes into view when you are almost right beside it. Tucked underneath a dramatic overhang of rock, it occupies a site which seems originally to have been used by a group of hermits. The story goes that its founder was a man from Zaragoza who, while hunting, was thrown off his horse and over the rock face; he was saved only on the intercession of St John, to whom he decided to dedicate the hermitage. In around 990 the original community was destroyed by the Moorish leader Almanzor, but was re-established 25 years later by King Sancho. The next 100 years represented the greatest period in the history of the monastery. The building was greatly favoured by the early Aragonese kings, who turned it into the spiritual centre of their kingdom, endowed it with relics and a great amount of money, and chose it as their burial-place. On 22 March 1071, for the first time in the history of the Spanish church, the Roman liturgy was used here rather than the Visigothic or Mozarabic one. At the same time the monastery adapted the Cluniac reforms, becoming one of the most important Spanish institutions to propagate these. Under Sancho Ramírez a new church was built above the old Mozarabic one, and the monastery was greatly extended. The subsequent dynasty of Aragonese rulers, beginning with Ramón Berenguer IV, did not have the same affection for the place as did their predecessors. None the less the place continued to function and to have additions made to it right until the end of the 17th century. A serious fire in 1675, combined with long-term problems of damp and falling rocks, led eventually to the abandonment of the monastery, and the creation of a new one on top of the Sierra; this in turn was sacked by the French at the beginning of the 19th century.

Exterior of San Juan de la Peña.

The 'old' monastery is on two levels, and the tour of the buildings begins with the lower of these. Passing through a large chamber which was probably a dormitory (it is erroneously known as the 'Sala del Concilio' on account of the romantic belief that an important meeting of church dignitaries took place here under Ramiro I), you will reach a small, narrow church comprising two aisles divided by wide arches. The western half is an extension dating from the 11th century, but the eastern one, divided by steps from the former, is a Mozarabic construction of probably 100 years earlier; it ends in twin niche-apses, hollowed into the rock, and covered with traces of Romanesque frescoes representing scenes from the life of Saints Cosmas and Damian.

Retracing your steps, you should now ascend to the upper level, where you will find the new church commissioned by Sancho Ramírez. Architecturally this is the most fascinating part of the whole complex, much of the interest being derived from the ingenious and evocative blending of natural and architectural forms. The memorable apsidal chapels, decorated with blind arcading, are carved out of the rock, while the roof of the wide single-aisled space in front is formed partially by the rock over-hang. Off the north side of the church is the narrow Pantheon of the Aragonese nobility, which was entirely rebuilt in the late 18th century, during the time of Charles III; the original tombs, looked after at that time by two monks from the upper monastery, were by then in a piteous state. The new Pantheon features large marble reliefs of scenes from Aragonese history, but the names of the illustrious Aragonese inscribed on the wall opposite probably bear little relation to the people actually buried here; some of the original, much restored tombs can be seen in a parallel gallery attached to the rock face.

The late Gothic portal of the Chapel of San Victorián, San Juan de la Peña.

The finest of the later additions to the monastery is the chapel of San Victorián on the south side of the church, built in the 1420s in a late Gothic style with rich vegetal motifs in the jambs of the arches. A Mozarabic horseshoe door on this same side leads from the church into the famous cloister, where most of the Romanesque sculptural decoration is concentrated. The free-standing arcade of the cloister, lying directly underneath the rock and commanding views out towards the Pyrenees, has been reassembled and restored at various times, most recently

The cloisters of San Juan de la Peña.

Capital of the Annunciation in the cloisters.

in the 1950s. The capitals, featuring scenes of the Old Testament and of the Life of Christ, as well as some purely fantastical motifs, are largely original, even though their present placing probably is not. The dating of these superlative works is highly controversial, and ranges from *c.* 1075 right up to 1200. The visit to San Juan de la Peña is completed by driving up to the late baroque 'new' monastery on top of the mountain. Occupying a green and wooded site very popular with picnickers and weekend excursionists, this vast complex has been left mainly in ruins, and adjoins an abandoned house with a reputation for being haunted. Only the monastery church has been well maintained. Its twin-towered west façade is typical of so much Spanish architecture in its placing of highly elaborate portals against a severe brick background.

LEYRE

Back on the N 240, you now follow one of the more monotonous stretches of the *Camino Aragonés*, a long flat stretch of road passing alongside abandoned hill-villages such as Berdun and Esco, reminders of Aragón's present status as the least populated of Spain's regions. Tiermas, mentioned in the *Codex Calixtinus* on account of its hot springs of Roman origin, now has only a handful of elderly people living there; its famous springs meanwhile disappeared with the building of the vast Yesa reservoir, which the road skirts for over 19 km

(12 miles). Running parallel to it on the other side of the road is the Sierra de Leyre, its summit marked by a long line of cliffs. Shortly after crossing the frontier of Navarre the pilgrims' route briefly leaves the N 240, and climbs up the Sierra to visit another monastery of great historical and architectural importance. The **Monastery of Leyre** is to Navarre what San Juan de la Peña is to Aragón, and, like the latter, enjoys a most exciting panorama, in this case embracing an apparently endless extent of mountains, valleys and vine-covered slopes. First mentioned in 848, when the Cordoban martyr Saint Eulogius referred to its rich library, it was chosen soon afterwards as the burial-place of the kings of Navarre. As with San Juan de la Peña, it enjoyed especial fame and privileges during the 11th century, when it too embraced the Cluniac reforms; it was the undisputed spiritual and cultural centre of Navarre, and its abbots served also as Bishops of Pamplona. However, with the brief union of Aragón and Navarre at the end of the century, it was neglected at the expense of San Juan de la Peña, and its decline was further hastened after the Cistercian reforms in the 13th century. Then, in 1954, following 118 years of abandonment, it was re-populated by Benedictine monks from Silos. Today it is a thriving monastic community, with an excellent hostelry and a reputation for its Gregorian chant: ideally you should try and come here in the evening to listen to the beautifully sung Vespers.

The negative aspect of the intensive restoration and rebuilding programme that took place at Leyre after the war is that most of the complex has from the outside a largely undistinguished look with the old parts squeezed between modern additions. Structurally the most interesting part of the church is the tall and elegant tri-apsidal east end, adjoining which are stairs leading down to the extraordinary crypt. The crypt, though consecrated in 1057, at the same time as the east end, seems much earlier in date, and has a most archaic appearance, very much as one would imagine the interior of some Celtic temple. It is one of the more unusual Romanesque structures in Spain, having tall and heavily built arches resting on large block-like capitals adorned with powerful but primitive carvings. Particularly strange is the way in which the capitals stand on shafts of unequal height, almost at ground level, as if pushed down by the weight of the arches.

The east end of the monastery church at Leyre.

To enter the upper church you have to walk along a neatly mown green space marking the site of the old cloister. The cloister was entered from the church through the latter's north portal, the simple decoration of which contrasts with the elaborate west portal. The latter, dating from the 12th century and known as the **Porta Speciosa**, has a tympanum featuring statues of Christ, the Virgin, St Peter and a Scribe; the arches above are covered all over with foliage and grotesques, while higher, in the spandrels, are representations of further saints, and scenes of the Visitation, the Annunciation, and the Martyrdom of Saints Nudilius and Alodia. The interior is especially light and harmonious — a wide, single-aisled space leading to an east wall perforated by three deep and barrel-vaulted apsidal chapels, the side ones being extremely narrow; the whole arrangement recalls the Lady Chapel at Cluny. Only the last three bays of the nave are Romanesque; the vaulting and the remaining bays are Gothic work of the 14th century. In a shallow, modern chapel leading from the otherwise bare north wall is the Pantheon of the Kings of Navarre, containing the tombs of two of the earliest Navarre kings — Sancho Carces (804–24), and Jimeno Iñiguez (824–82). After leaving the church you can walk to the legendary fountain where one of the abbots, enchanted by the sound of a bird, is supposed to have spent 300 years asleep.

After descending from Leyre to the village of Yesa, you may either continue along the N 240, or else make a small detour to include Sangüesa, one of the first Spanish towns to be developed as a result of the pilgrim traffic. If you chose the latter route you will also see Javier, a place which became a pilgrimage centre in its own right after the 16th century, for it was here, in 1506, that the Jesuit missionary Francis Xavier was born. The family of St Francis were the lords of the village and responsible for the 16th-century castle which now dominates the place. This crenellated structure was heavily restored this century, and given a Disneyland appearance, as well as an unappealing Neo-Gothic church. The actual church where St Francis was baptized is a very simple medieval building directly in front of the castle, and is now attached to a modest covent.

Sangüesa is in many ways the most attractive and best preserved of all the towns on the *Camino Aragonés*. Originally built as a hillside settlement (to be identified with the village now known as Rocaforte), it moved to the present location on the banks of the River Aragón in the late 11th century, during the reign of Sancho Ramírez. Ramírez, keen to promote both the pilgrimge and trade links with France, encouraged French settlers to move here. He himself had a palace built here, and around this grew the nucleus of the town. Its rapid growth was briefly interrupted after 1134 when Navarre broke with Aragón, but soon afterwards the town revived as a result of the influx of a number of religious orders, and of its being chosen as a residence both by the kings of Navarre and the Navarrese nobility. Today Sangüesa is a lively small town, with numerous medieval churches and elegant palaces.

The first important building to be seen by pilgrims on their way through was the **Church of Santiago**, which is right in the centre of the old town. Begun in around 1120 it was largely completed by the late 13th century; its tall, sturdy belfry, which dwarfs the building and gives it a fortress-like appearance, was given its crenellations around 1365. Only the tri-apsidal east end — a variant of that of Jaca cathedral — is Romanesque, and until very recently this was completely hidden on the outside by latter additions; even today a large 18th-century altarpiece makes it difficult to appreciate the interior of the main apse. In 1964 a late 13th-century statue of St James dressed as a pilgrim was placed on the plainly decorated Gothic west façade, and there are further emblems of the pilgrimage carved on the charming parish house on the opposite side of the square.

Sanqüesa: the west portal of the Church of Santiago, with 13th-century statue of St James dressed as a pilgrim.

Due north of the church, along the Rua de Santiago, you come to the **Rua Mayor**, the oldest and most important street of Sangüesa. Pilgrims headed west along it, passing shortly on their right what was up to 1570 the south wing of the Royal Palace. In 1570 this wing was pulled down to build the arcaded **Town Hall**, which is fringed by richly carved and exceptionally wide eaves, the latter being very characteristic of post-medieval architecture in Navarre. You can walk through the ground floor arcade of the Town Hall into a small and delightful tree-lined square, which was originally the courtyard of the Royal Palace. The surviving north wing of the palace, dating back to the 11th century but heavily modified by the Navarre kings in the 13th and 14th centuries, was originally attached to the town walls: it comprises a central block pierced by paired Romanesque windows and flanked by imposing crenellated towers. Continuing west along the Rua Mayor, you will pass at Nos 14 and 12 the adjoining palaces of Guendulaín and Granada, two of the most impressive secular buildings in the town. Both are of brick and protected by wide eaves, the latter palace having also elaborate late Gothic windows.

Finally you reach the church of **Santa María la Real**, which stands above the river Aragón, next to the medieval bridge by which the pilgrims left Sangüesa. Begun in the early 12th

Sanqüesa: the south portal of Santa María la Real.

century, this church has a tri-apsidal Romanesque east end comparable to that of Jaca cathedral, but perfectly preserved and with finely carved corbels and capitals, one of which charmingly represents the Flight into Egypt. The rest of the fabric was completed by the end of the 12th century, with the exception of the splendid octagonal tower, which was begun around the middle of the following century, and not given its spire and crenellated upper level until after 1365. The spire lends the church a strong French character, and indeed French artists seem to have worked on this building. French influence is most obviously apparent in the magnificent south portal, which is one of the most elaborate and interesting 12th-century portals along the whole *Camino Francés*. The six columns that support the tentatively Gothic arch are adorned with six elongated figures representing, from left to right, Mary

Magdalene, the Virgin, the mother of St James, St Paul, St Peter and the hanged Judas. The artist was one Leodegarius, whose signature (*Leodagarius me fecit*) appears in the book held by the Virgin; nothing else is known about this man, but it is assumed that the artist must be French, as the works are clearly inspired by the mid-12th-century figures that feature on the royal portal of Chartres cathedral. The tympanum, representing The Last Judgement, recalls instead Romanesque works in Moissac and elsewhere in south-western France; an exceptionally lively range of carvings proliferates in iconographical chaos all over the covings and spandrels, contrasting with the very static figures of God, the Four Evangelists and the Twelve Apostles that stand in two superimposed rows of arcading at the very top of the portal (these latter works, clearly by a different hand, are thought by some to be by the Master of San Juan de la Peña). The interest of the dark interior lies essentially in the Gothic vaulting, particularly that of the crossing dome, which rests on squinches. The main Romanesque section of the building — the sanctuary — has piers with unusually-shaped capitals, but its space is difficult to appreciate owing to its being largely hidden by an enormous Renaissance High Altar. A curiosity of the church is the well in the south-west corner: its presence is explained by the fact that pilgrims were once accommodated within the building.

MONREAL AND EUNATE

The pilgrims' route through Javier and Sangüesa rejoins the main Pamplona road 5 km (3 miles) after crossing the Aragón. You now follow the main road until shortly after Monreal, a village which Picaud designated as the beginning of the third and final stage of the *Camino Aragonés*. The old centre of Monreal, bypassed by the main road, is without any special architectural merit, though a short detour can be recommended to see the well-preserved medieval **Bridge**, which lies neglected at the bottom of the village and was once used by pilgrims. Turning west off the N 240 on to the small NA 500, you enter a hilly, fertile and intensely green landscape so typical of much of Navarre. The last stretch of the *Camino Aragonés* before reaching Puente la Reina takes you through a particularly luscious valley, in the middle of which, standing in evocative isolation among fields is the fascinating **Church of**

Eunate. This is one of a handful of octagonal Romanesque buildings to be found in Spain. Imitative of the Holy Roman Sepulchre of Jerusalem, they are usually associated with the Templars, who indeed flourished in Navarre under the rule of King Sancho the Wise (1150–94). However, this particular building, though clearly influenced by Templar architecture, was not a Templar church, as is so often said, but a pilgrims' burial place connecting with a hospital belonging to the order of St John of Jerusalem. There are some worn heads around the exterior, and further carvings on the north portal and inside the small rib-vaulted chancel attached to the octagon. Rib-vaulting covers the octagon itself, a large and barely decorated space, pleasingly light and simple. Of especial interest, and the subject of much discussion, is the free-standing arcading which surrounds the building and recalls the porticoes of the Temple Platform in Jerusalem. Whether it served any particular function is not known.

The church of Eunate.

31

NAVARRE
VALCARLOS TO VIANA

The majority of pilgrims to Santiago have always crossed the Pyrenees over the Valcarlos Pass, which is lower than that of Somport and has a rather gentler and less sinister look. This alternative route to the *Camino Aragonés* is called the *Camino Navarro* and takes you through the heart of the former kingdom of Navarre, a region now divided between France and Spain and which extends almost all the way to the Rioja town of Logroño.

The people of Navarre share a common ancestry with the Basques, their land having once belonged to the Vascons, who had fled to the northern half of their territory and to the adjoining region now known as the Basque Country following the Moorish invasion of Spain. The Navarrese are sometimes described by other Spaniards as being crude and unsophisticated, though few people today would express such an opinion with quite the same vigour as did Aymeric Picaud, who reserved for them some of the cruellest criticisms of his *Pilgrims' Guide*. For Picaud the Navarrese dressed as badly as the Scots and made sounds while eating comparable to those of 'dogs or pigs gulping gluttonously'; they were, he summed up,

> a barbarous race, different from most others and by their customs and race full of wickedness, black in colour, with ugly faces, debauched, perverse, perfidious, disloyal, corrupt, drunkards, expert in all deeds of violence, fierce and savage, dishonest and false, impious and rude, cruel and quarrelsome, incapable of any decent sentiment and used to every vice and iniquity.

On the positive side they were 'good on the battlefield', and indeed at Roncesvalles, the first place of major interest on the *Camino Navarro*, they were responsible in 778 for one of the most important defeats in Charlemagne's career. Their victory here is not acknowledged in the famous *Song of Roland*, which describes this battle simply as a skirmish with the Moors in which the heroic Roland was killed.

(Opposite) The cloisters and church of San Pedro de la Rua, Estella.

It was shortly after the victory at Roncesvalles that the kingdom of Navarre was created, with Pamplona as its capital. The kingdom flourished in the 11th century, especially under the rule of Sancho III the Great (1000–35), who dreamt of uniting Christian Spain, and under whose rule the *Camino Francés* was firmly established. Divided on his death between his four sons, Navarre did not survive long as a great and independent kingdom, being annexed to Aragón in 1074. It was ruled again by its own kings after 1134, but its throne was occupied in 1234 by Thibaud I of Champagne, who initiated a succession of French dynasties which was to last until 1512. These centuries of French rule, however, though marked by continual tensions between the local nobility and the foreign monarchs, represented by no means a period of cultural decline. Whereas the Aragonese district of Jaca stagnated both politically and culturally after around 1200, Navarre expe-

The pilgrims' way from Valcarlos to Viana.

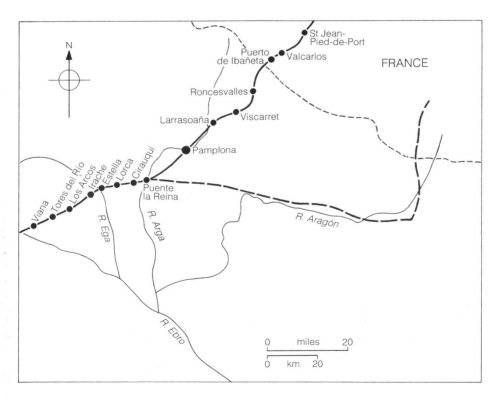

rienced a period of enormous artistic activity, which reached
its zenith during the reign of Charles III, the Noble
(1387–1425), a man responsible for the building of countless
churches and castles; Navarre became after the 13th century
one of the main Spanish centres for the transmission of French
Gothic art and architecture.

In 1512 Navarre was siezed for the crown of Spain, and
thereafter only the small part of this region to the east of the
Pyrenees (the so-called Lower Navarre) was to be once more in
French possession. The Navarrese always maintained a certain
distance from the rest of Spain, and continued to enjoy long
after the unification municipal privileges that had been
granted to them in the early Middle Ages; the pride of these
people is proverbial, and it was in an attempt to curtail this that
Cardinal Cisneros, in the early 16th century, lopped off the
upper layers of many of their church and palace towers. In the
19th century, Navarre became a great bastion of the Carlist
cause, and, in more recent times, the place has emerged as a
thriving centre of the Basque terrorist organisation known as
ETA, the aims of which are the political independence not only
of the Basque Country but also of Northern Navarre; several
of the villages that you pass on the *Camino Navarro* in between
the French frontier and Pamplona are notorious terrorist hide-
outs.

ST JEAN-PIED-DE-PORT AND THE VALCARLOS PASS

Those who follow the *Camino Navarro* generally begin their
journey at the small French town of St Jean-Pied-de-Port,
where for many years the celebrated Madame Debril has been
offering travellers to Santiago special passports and a warm
send-off. The look of this town — the capital of Lower
Navarre — is similar to that of many villages on the Spanish
side of the frontier, the houses being characterized by their
white walls, stone quoins, and steeply pitched slate roofs.
From St Jean-Pied-de-Port the climb begins up the Valcarlos
Pass. Travellers on foot should, in good weather, avoid the
main road, and take the Route de Napoléon, a track of Roman
origin which leads directly from the village to Roncesvalles,
and has wonderfully extensive views. The landscape has not
the bare and savage appearance which you find around
Somport, but is remarkably green, and becomes even more so

as you descend into the Valley of Valcarlos, a rolling landscape of meadows, oaks, pines and chestnuts, with roads lined with rows of trees reminiscent of France. The *Camino Navarro* up to Pamplona does not offer the architectural interest of the *Camino Aragonés*, and even Roncesvalles itself is more fascinating for its historical associations than its architecture.

The *Song of Roland* is recalled in a small modern memorial 1 km (½ mile) east of the monastery of Roncesvalles; a chapel of 1964 marks the site of a medieval cross commemorating the supposed place where Charlemagne fell to his knees and prayed towards Santiago. Around the chapel once stood the important monastery of San Salvador, which dated back at least to the mid-11th century and which continued to offer hospitality to pilgrims right up to the 17th century; after a fitful history it was destroyed once and for all by fire in 1884, and today only the scant ruins of its 19th-century buildings survive. The nearby monastery of Roncesvalles, founded by the bishop of Pamplona in the mid-12th century, had in any case soon superseded San Salvador in importance. Richly endowed by monarchs and pilgrims from all over Europe, it could boast by the 13th century a pilgrims' hospital and hostelry rivalling those of Somport; the monastery continues to flourish today, and to be run by Augustinian monks.

RONCESVALLES

Roncesvalles is one of the major tourist attractions of the pilgrims' way and swarms with visitors in the summer months. The verdant, wooded setting is very appealing, and in the monastery's small museum are kept some beautiful and fascinating objects associated with Charlemagne, most notably a square enamel reliquary of the 12th century nicknamed 'Charlemagne's Chess-set'. However, the rather cold and forbidding monastic buildings, with their steep, pitched, grey zinc roofs, are somewhat disappointing, having been rebuilt and restored at numerous stages in history. The oldest building is the curious funerary chapel, which stands outside the main complex, supposedly on the spot where Roland was buried; resembling more a medieval market than a chapel, this rectangular building is surrounded on all sides by arcading, though virtually nothing of the fabric is original. You walk through a large 18th-century courtyard to reach the monastery's museum, cloister and collegiate church. The small Gothic cloister, an austere undecorated space, was reconstructed around 1600, but in the middle has been placed a 12th-century Baptismal font. The former 14th-century **Chapter-house**, which stands off the cloister, was transformed in 1912 into a pantheon housing the tomb of Sancho VII the Strong; the base is modern, but the tomb itself is a fine 13th-century work, 2.25 m (over 7 ft) long, the size apparently of the king himself. Apart from his size, Sancho's main claim to fame was to have taken part in the victorious battle of 1212 against the Moors at Navas de Tolosa in Andalucía; a large stained-glass window of 1912 commemorates the event, and you can also see in the chapel the chains that surrounded the tent of the Moorish king Miramolín and that were broken by Sancho during the battle (these chains were later incorporated into the coat of arms of Navarre). The **Collegiate Church**, on a higher level than the cloister, was begun in 1195 and completed in 1215, but rebuilt in a high Gothic style after a fire in 1400, and restored several times since then; the crude restoration programme which is continuing at present threatens to deprive the building completely of all remaining medieval character. The main interest of the interior for pilgrims is the miraculous statue of the Virgin, a medieval work displayed under a modern *baldacchino* above the high altar.

As you continue heading west towards Pamplona the landscape becomes ever more verdant until eventually you descend into the exceptionally fertile plain which surrounds the capital city of Navarre. Originally a Vascon settlement, Pamplona was refounded by Pompey in *c*. 77 BC and given the name Pompelo or Pompeiopolis. Captured by the Moors in around 732, it was later taken by Charlemagne, whose destruction of the city's walls led to the Navarrese retaliation at Roncesvalles in 778. During the reign of Sancho III in the early 10th century, the city began to develop rapidly, and an important new district soon rose up, centred around the church of San Cernin and populated mainly by French and other merchants. The process of expansion intensified in the course of the 13th and 14th centuries, and further French settlers led to the creation of the so-called New Town, which was later known as the district of

San Nicolás. The main districts of Pamplona were separated from each other by walls and enjoyed different privileges, dependant either on the Crown or on the Church. This led to much rivalry and hostility, and the situation worsened after the annexation of Navarre to Castile in 1512, when the predominantly French districts of San Cernin and San Nicolás were in near continual conflict with the Castillian district centred around the cathedral. The Navarrese French, aided by troops from France, made several attempts to recapture Pamplona; in the siege of 1521 one of the Castillian soldiers wounded was the young Ignatius Loyola, who profited from his period of convalescence by devising the Jesuit order. In 1571 Philip II had a new citadel built, and there was extensive rebuilding and new development in the 18th and 19th centuries, leading to the pulling down of most of the medieval walls and the creation of a large new town comprising a regular grid of long and wide avenues. The local economy has been based throughout the centuries on agriculture, and the city has been scarcely affected by heavy industry.

For all its sprouting modern suburbs, the beauty of Pamplona's surroundings is still very much apparent, and the place makes a particularly striking impression when approached on the pilgrims' way, its extensive remaining ramparts rising up on a green and sharp escarpment above the wooded banks of the river Arga. If on foot, you cross the river on the 14th-century **Magdalena Bridge**, and then enter the old town through the **Portal de Francia**, the best preserved of Pamplona's medieval gates. The stretch of walls in between this gate and the **Museum of Navarre** has gardens at its foot and a public promenade commanding views towards the Pyrenees that were described by the English Neo-Gothic architect G.E. Street as being 'eminently lovely'; the Museum itself, imaginatively and spaciously housed in a 16th-century hospital, is well worth a visit for its large collection of medieval wall paintings from the region and for its remarkably intricate and delicate Romanesque capitals originating from the cathedral's cloister.

If instead of turning right at the Portal de Francia in the direction of the Museum of Navarre, you turned left, you would enter the oldest part of Pamplona, a district known as the **Navarrería** and populated in the Middle Ages largely by

Castillians, among whom were the workers involved in the
construction of the cathedral. The **Cathedral** dominates this
district of dark and narrow streets, and stands near to the
ramparts. The original Romanesque structure was pulled
down in the late 14th century, during the reign of Charles III,
and replaced by the present Gothic one, which was completed
around 1525. Apart from the capitals in the Museum of
Navarre, all that was kept of the Romanesque cathedral was
the west façade, which had apparently numerous carvings of
naked men and women placed, in the words of one English
traveller of 1768, 'in such postures, as it is not fit to tell'.
However, even this was later demolished, and in its stead there
was put up, in 1783, during what Richard Ford described as
the 'pseudo-classical and royal Academic mania', the present
monstrously over-blown and singularly humourless Corinthian structure by Ventura Rodriguez. After this pompous
entrance, the harmonious, uncluttered and relatively small
cathedral interior comes as a pleasant relief. The overall effect
is relatively severe and heavy, with a large expanse of bare
masonry in the place of a triforium gallery. G.E. Street

Pamplona cathedral
cloisters — detail of
tracery.

39

Pamplona cathedral:
the cloisters.

commented on the insignificance of the mouldings in
comparison to the large size of the columns, and found that the
consequent lack 'of bold light and shade' was indicative of the
decline of the Gothic style in the 15th century. Street's views on
the cathedral were in fact ambivalent, and he had mixed praise
for the curious apse, which has only two canted sides, their
arches springing from a central column placed behind the high
altar; for Street one of the advantages of such an arrangement
was that a characteristically tall Spanish altarpiece could be
placed in front of the apse with minimum interference with the
architecture. The appearance of the chevet has changed
somewhat since Street's day owing to the recent moving there
from the nave of the Renaissance choir.

One of the great sculptural treasures of the interior is the early 15th-century tomb of Charles III and his queen, Leonor of Castille; this alabaster work, standing in the right transept, is by the Tournai artist Jean de Lomme, and is notable for its Burgundian realism, which is evident in particular in the numerous figures of mourners that surround the base. But it is the cathedral's early 15th-century **Cloisters** which provide the building's greatest treat. They have been unfailingly praised by visitors, including Victor Hugo, who wrote of them that 'everything here is beautiful — the dimensions and proportions, the form and the colour, the overall unity and the detail, the light and the shadow'. Of exceptionally delicate appearance — in contrast to the cathedral's interior — they comprise tall arches pierced by tracery which extends over the balustrade on the cloister's upper level and up into a series of sharply pointed gables; the sun shining through the tracery creates magical effects of lace-like intricacy. The sculptural decoration of the cloisters is suitably exquisite, in particular that on the south side decorating the so-called **Puerta Preciosa**, a portal flanked by statues of the Virgin and the angel of the annunciation, and bearing a tympanum carved with scenes from the life of the Virgin. The Diocesan museum which lies off the cloisters is housed in a refectory which was once used both by canons and pilgrims.

The traditional pilgrims' route through Pamplona led due west of the cathedral, down the Calles Curia and Mercaderes, and into the district of San Cernin. At the end of the Calle Mercaderes, at the point where Pamplona's three main districts met, a town hall was built in the early 15th century — the idea being to celebrate a treaty of 1423 intended to unite these districts. This building was in ruins by the mid-18th century, and a new town hall was erected, of which today only the façade survives; this tall, tiered and elaborate façade, one of the finest of the city's many 18th-century structures, is very reminiscent in its proportions and detailing to buildings of the Flemish baroque. The church of **San Saturnino**, the parish church of the Cernin district, stands on a cramped adjoining site where Saint Saturninus is said to have baptized the first Christians of Pamplona (the exact spot where he preached is marked by a plaque in front of the building). Pilgrims seem to have had a special affection for this church, and there is a

statue of Saint James above the main entrance; it is also thought that the Romanesque building over which the present structure was built was inspired by the celebrated pilgrimage church of Saint Sernin in Toulouse. The rebuilding took place at the end of the 13th century and gave the church a fortress-like appearance, complete with two tall crenellated towers; the crenellations have now been replaced by ugly lanterns, and the church has been subjected to many other modifications, including the destruction of the cloister to make way for the cavernous 18th-century chapel of the Virgen del Camino.

The pilgrims' route west of Pamplona, essentially follows the main road to Burgos, the N 111, though for those who are walking, there are long stretches of footpath parallel to the road. The exact meeting-place of the *Camino Aragonés* and the *Camino Navarro* has been the subject of much rivalry between the neighbouring villages of Obanos and Puente la Reina, situated respectively 40 and 43 km (25 and 28 miles) west of Pamplona; the dispute remains unresolved, and there are modern monuments commemorating the pilgrimage on the outskirts of both villages. At all events Puente la Reina, the richer of the two places architecturally, grew up as a result of the great confluence of pilgrims from the two branches of the *Camino Francés*. Occupying a pleasant situation on the fertile banks of the River Arga, it is an excellently preserved village highly evocative of the early days of the pilgrimage, and built up alongside the old pilgrims' route, the Rua Mayor (the N 111 bypasses the old centre). At the eastern end of the village is the **Iglesia del Crucifijo**, which was once attached to a medieval monastery and pilgrims' hostel, but is now joined by an arch to the 18th-century Convento de los Reparadores. The church comprises in fact two connected churches, the earlier of the two being a late Romanesque structure entered through a southern portal richly carved — possibly by Moorish crafts-men — with scallop-shells and grotesque beasts. The first building soon proved too small to accommodate the ever-growing number of pilgrims to the town, and was extended by pulling down the north wall and adding a 14th-century Gothic wing; it is in this later part of the church that is kept the Y-shaped and very expressive carved wood **Crucifix** which was

PUENTE LA
REINA

(Opposite) Pamplona: the portal on the north side of the cathedral cloisters with tympanum representing the Dormition of the Virgin.

43

Puente la Reina: the south portal of the Church of Santiago.

Puente la Reina: the medieval bridge.

reputedly brought here by a pilgrim from Germany, and which gives the church its name.

The quiet and dark Rua Mayor (which is also known as the 'Rua de los Romeros', or 'Pilgrims' route') is lined for almost its whole length by buildings dating from the medieval to late baroque periods. A third of the way down, on the right-hand side, is the **Church of Santiago**, which has an elaborately carved, if rather worn, Romanesque portal, the cusped arches of which give it a strong Moorish character (the only other two churches in Navarre with such arches are to be seen further along the pilgrims' way). The portal is the only survival of the original 12th-century church, the rest of the fabric being mainly of the early 16th century, with the exception of the tall bell-tower, an 18th-century work by Ventura Rodriguez. The single-aisled interior has complex late Gothic vaulting spring-ing from plain, unfaced stone walls. The furnishings are largely baroque, but there are two superlative 14th-century statues near the entrance: one is of St Bartholomew and is in polychromed stone, the other is in polychromed wood and represents St James dressed as a pilgrim. The highly polished floor consists entirely of wooden tombs, a feature peculiar to this part of Spain.

The Rua Mayor, after passing alongside a small square once used for bull-fights, comes to an end at a medieval gateway placed in front of the famous **Bridge** after which the town is named. This bridge, now used only by pedestrians and animals, is a six-arched construction dating back to the early

11th century, and as such, one of the most important surviving Romanesque bridges of the pilgrims' way. Once across it you find yourself in open countryside, and there are excellent views back to the village. The tranquility of the river's banks must once have been deceptive, for, according to Picaud, the water here was poisonous, and Navarrese men with sharpened knives waited in keen anticipation for pilgrims' horses to drop dead so that they could flay them.

The pilgrims' route continues though green and rolling landscape studded with vines for the remainder of the journey through Navarre. After the village of Mañeru, where there is the amusing sight of a modest Romanesque chapel converted into an equally humble cinema, the old pilgrims' path deviates slightly from the main road to climb up to the enchanting hill-village of Cirauqui. Though signs of tourist exploitation in the form of the odd crafts shop are beginning to be evident, Cirauqui still manages to retain a remarkably authentic medieval character, and has narrow lanes lined with imposing stone houses and palaces, many of which bear prominent heraldic crests. At the top of the village is the 13th-century church of **San Román**, the second of the Navarre churches to have a multi-lobed main portal, in this case one of Gothic shape. As you leave the village and slowly descend its hill, the feeling of having been in a place which has changed little over the centuries is reinforced by your having to walk over a path which is still laid with some of its original Roman stones.

CIRAUQUI

The town of Estella, one of the highpoints of the pilgrims' way through Navarre, has been recognized for its beauty since the Middle Ages, when it was dubbed by pilgrims as 'Estella la Bella'. Even Aymeric Picaud, so caustic about Navarre generally, managed a rare moment of enthusiasm for the town, praising it as a place 'where the bread is good, the wine excellent, the meat and fish are abundant, and which enjoys all delights'; as late as 1592 the courtier Enrique Cock could write that he knew of 'no better place in the whole of Spain'. Travellers visiting the place today, after reading such descriptions, might be disappointed by the rather run-down

ESTELLA

look of parts of the town and by some of the more tasteless modern additions, but there is no denying Estella's remarkable concentration of medieval monuments.

A place of ancient origin, mentioned by Ptolomey and Strabo, Estella was given a renewed importance in the late 11th century, when Sancho Ramírez decided to repopulate it with French settlers, for whom a new district was created on the left bank of the river Ega. Turned the following century into a royal residence by the Kings of Navarre, the town flourished more than ever, and it continued to prosper after the annexation of the region to Castile, thanks to the wealth of its agriculture and its reputation as a centre of crafts, printing, and the manufacturing of religious artefacts. Unlike most other towns in this part of Navarre, which occupy prominent hill-top positions, Estella is hidden in a narrow valley, and only comes into view at close quarters. The original settlement, on the right bank of the Ega, was built around a rocky spur which was later crowned by the church of **San Miguel**. This church, reached by a magnificent medieval flight of steps, is interesting above all for its Romanesque north portal, the oldest surviving part of the building. The outstanding carvings on the portal feature a typanum of Christ in Majesty bearing the strange inscription: 'the image which you see is neither God nor Man, but God and Man are represented by this holy image'. Flanking the arch are carved reliefs executed with extreme boldness, the one on the right portraying the Three Marys at the Tomb, and that on the left The Descent into Limbo and St Michael Weighing the Souls. What you see today is sadly only a fragment of a much larger whole, the upper part of the façade having been destroyed in 1512. The rest of this fortress-like church is mainly in a transitional Gothic style, though the building is at present undergoing much needed restoration and cannot be seen.

The lively centre of present-day Estella extends to the north of San Miguel, the main square being the attractively arcaded **Plaza de Santiago**. There are several interesting buildings in this part of town, such as the neo-Moorish bus station, the heavily restored and much altered church of **San Juan Bautista** (founded in 1187), and the small and out-of-the-way **San Pedro de Lizarra**, a 14th-century structure (with a tall 16th-century tower) built over what was probably the oldest church in

Estella: the Plaza de San Martín, featuring the Palace of the Kings of Navarre on right, and the Church of San Pedro la Rua in background.

Estella. But the main monument of interest for pilgrims on this side of the River Ega was the **Basilica of Nuestra Señora del Puy**, which stands on a wooded site above the town, and provides the finest overall view of Estella. The much venerated image of the Virgin which is kept here is generally thought to be a French work of the 13th and 14th centuries, but there are some who maintain that it is a Visigothic piece; the miracle which it inspired is at any rate supposed to have taken place in 1085, conveniently just in time for the re-population of the town by Sancho Ramírez. The original building which housed it has long since gone, and was replaced in 1951 by a controversial star-shaped structure in glass and concrete.

The pilgrims' route through Estella lingered only shortly on the right bank of the Ega, then crossed the river by a bridge just below San Miguel, reaching the part of town which had been settled by the French. It is in this now quiet and strangely neglected district that most of Estella's most interesting buildings are to be seen. The main street here is the Calle de la Rua, which runs parallel to the river and leads to the Plaza de San Martín, the heart of the medieval town. Following this street in the other direction, and passing underneath the modern Puente de San Agustín, you will come to the Calle Curtidores, where you will find, surrounded by dereliction, the church of **Santo Sepulcro**. This former burial place of the French population of Estella has a Romanesque apse of the early 13th century, but its principal attraction is the west

Estella: detail showing a lintel support from the main portal of Santo Sepulcro.

47

façade of 1328, paid for by the merchants of the district. The wide Gothic arch which dominates the portal has a tympanum featuring the Crucifixion and an especially lively representation of the Last Supper; Old Testament figures are wittily shown supporting the lintel with their hands. On either side of the door are statues of an unknown bishop or abbot and St James as a pilgrim, while above, flanking the arch itself, are trefoiled niches containing the apostles. The façade has a truncated look, and indeed, like that of San Miguel was reduced in size by Castillian troops after 1512; the church itself was deconsecrated in 1881, and has been closed for many years while awaiting conversion into a small archaeological museum. Behind the building once stood the walls of the town's Jewish ghetto, which dates back to at least 1093, and was considerably expanded after 1492, when the King of Navarre, defending the Jews as a 'gentle and reasonable race', welcomed those who had been expelled from Spain by Ferdinand and Isabel. The tiny church of **Santa María Jus del Castillo**, with a 12th-century apse, was used as a synagogue up to 1145, and is the only remaining memento of the former ghetto. Adjoining this is the large **Monastery of Santo Domingo**, founded in the 13th century by King Theobald II, and recently transformed into an old people's home; earlier this century the great Catalan muralist José María Sert had contemplated acquiring the place as a studio. You should ask at the reception desk for the keys to the now abandoned monastery church, a majestic, single-aisled structure in a Cistercian Gothic style.

Walking west along the Calle de la Rua towards the Plaza de San Martín, you will pass on your right, shortly before reaching the square, the **Palacio de Fray Diego** (now the Casa de Cultura), a graceful Renaissance building with a two-storeyed patio featuring windows framed by plateresque grotesques. A few yards further along, on the other side of the road, is the former **Town Hall**, built in the 16th century over the church of San Martín, which is where the pilgrims and French residents of the town once used to gather. The building overlooks to the west the small Plaza de San Martín, which is centred around a 16th-century fountain and is the most beautiful and best preserved corner of old Estella. Shielded by a line of trees on the opposite side to the former Town Hall, is

the **Palace of the Kings of Navarre**, a 12th-century palace built
by Sancho the Wise. Though it has been extensively restored
and retains relatively little of its original masonry, it can still
claim to be one of the most important examples of Romanesque civic architecture in Europe. Its finest façade is its
northern one, overlooking the street of San Nicolás, and
comprising a ground floor loggia and an upper level featuring
a row of small four-arched openings. One of the capitals in the
upper level has a wonderful carving of monsters and the
damned, but the most famous sculptural work on the building
is the capital on the loggia representing Roland's battle with
the monster Ferragut; this work, based on a version of the
Roland legend attributed to the 12th-century Archbishop
Turpin, is signed by one Martin of Logroño.

Rising up at the top of a tall flight of steps on the north side of the square, and set against a background of wooded slopes, is the 12th-century church of **San Pedro de la Rua**; its restored bell-tower thrusts high above it and clearly shows, in its prominent masonry break, the level to which it was once reduced by Cardinal Cisneros. The magnificent west portal features the third and last of the polylobed arches that you will see in Navarre; there is no tympanum, but instead much carving on the covings and capitals, including fantastical animals of Moorish inspiration, like the arch itself. The tri-apsidal east end is the oldest and least altered part of the interior, and in its central section has the curious feature of a row of 'minor apses' on the lower level, indication presumably of an earlier plan. A door in the second bay to the right leads into the celebrated Romanesque cloisters, surrounded by paired columns supporting delicately carved capitals, including representations of the Apocalypse, and of the lives of Christ, St Andrew, St Peter and St Lawrence. The west side of the cloisters has vegetal and animal motifs comparable to those in Moorish tapestries, suggesting that Moorish craftsmen worked here as well as on the building's west portal.

IRACHE

Heading west along the Calle San Nicolás, the pilgrims' route leaves the old town by way of the Puerta de Castilla, Estella's main surviving medieval gate. Soon it regains the main Burgos road, passing on the right the prominently sited **Palace of Luquin**, an early 17th-century building recently restored and relocated, and now used by the Fisios Institute, one of Spain's leading homeopathic clinics. Just outside the town is the former **Monastery of Irache**, reputedly one of the oldest Benedictine foundations in Spain, though not documented before 958. Richly endowed by Sancho the Great in the early 11th century, it acquired soon afterwards a pilgrims' hospital; but it was not until the end of the 11th century, under the leadership of Saint Veremundus, that it was to enter the most important period in its history. The decline set in during the 13th century, but the monastery prospered once more after 1522, with the setting up of a teaching establishment which was to acquire the status of university in 1615. Abandoned finally in the 19th century, it has only been restored in recent years.

The monastery church, begun in the second half of the 12th century in a pure Romanesque style, was largely completed in a transitional Gothic one early the following century. Altered and added to in the 16th century and later, it has a west façade which brings together three radically different styles. The main portal, shielded by a narthex, is transitional Gothic work of the late 12th century, while above this is a fanciful baroque addition of the 18th century; finally, to the left of the portal, is a bell-tower of 1609 clearly inspired by the austere geometry of Juan de Herrera's Palace and Monastery of El Escorial near Madrid. Slightly later in date than the tower, but in a comparably austere style is the large 17th-century wing attached to the church. The entrance to the monastery is through the main door of this wing, and takes you at first into a large cloister in a severly classical style. Beyond is a Renaissance cloister, begun in 1545, but not completed until the end of the 16th century. Elaborate late Gothic vaulting rests on capitals of classical inspiration, and, as so often happens in the 16th century, mythological and pagan motifs mingle with religious ones; the overall effect is very rich, and would have been even more so had not French soldiers stolen the figures that once stood in the niches that decorate the columns and walls. A particularly fine classical plateresque door, shaped like a triumphal arch and adorned with classical medallions, leads from the cloisters into the church. A very different architecture awaits you inside, the simplicity and purity of which are particularly apparent owing to the removal in the last century of the profusely gilded Renaissance altars and other furnishings (these can now be seen in the nearby parish church of Dicastillo). The three apses, unencumbered now by later additions and obstructions, are in a pure Romanesque style, the central apse articulated by blind arcading and decorated with only the simplest of decorative motifs. The raised choir in the west end, and the crossing dome are of the Renaissance, but the rest of the church is of the Cistercian period, with quadripartite vaulting sprung from a giant order of columns, and with transepts extending no further than the aisles; everything is beautifully proportioned and in perfect harmony. The north portal, overlooking the monastery's gardens has worn capitals carved with hunting scenes and fantastical animals.

LOS ARCOS AND TORRES DEL RÍO	The next monument of interest along the pilgrims' route is at Los Arcos, 17 km (10 miles) away. This small town, at one time a residence of Charles III of Navarre, is today a largely unappealing place, sprawled out along the busy N 111. However, set back slightly from the main road, is a small and pleasant arcaded square dominated by the impressively tall **Parish Church**. The church's north portal, shaded by a large portico, is a classical plateresque work, while the soaring bell-tower is an elegant baroque construction with a Gothic-inspired lantern incorporating tracery, buttresses and cylindrical turrets. The interior is as chaotic as that of Irache is pure and restful, and brings together a confusing mixture of Renaissance, baroque and late Gothic elements. Dark and gloomy, and with vaulting covered in stucco and blackened 18th-century frescoes, its main note of colour is provided by its dazzlingly gilded and startling baroque altars. The more puritanically-minded might prefer the late Gothic cloisters on the south side of the church.

Adjoining the church is the **Puerta de Castilla**, an early 17th-century gate through which pilgrims left the town. The old route runs parallel to the main road, crossing a landscape of vines before ascending to the village of Sansol, from where there is a sharp and impressive view down to Torres del Río, a well-preserved medieval village thrust up above the tree-lined Linares River. The main attraction of Torres is the tiny 12th-century **Church of the Holy Sepulchre**. The special feature of this building is not its octagonal shape — which is common to most Templar churches, and, of course, is to be found at Eunate — but the way in which its cross-ribbed vaults are so placed as to form a central lantern, a type of vaulting characteristic of Moorish Spain, and which was later to be taken up by the Italian baroque architect Guarino Guarini; there are few better examples in Spain of the adaptation by Christians of Moorish building techniques.

VIANA	The small town of Viana, straddling a low hill just off the N 111, is a frontier town with Castile, and was heavily fortified. The line of the old fortifications is clearly apparent, and several of the original gates have survived. Within the walls is a place

of considerable character, with narrow streets lined with old places that recall Viana's past as a capital of a small principality founded by Charles III as an apanage for his heirs. Though Viana was a major stop on the pilgrims' route, there is no surviving monument attesting to the pilgrimage in medieval times — the earliest testimony is a baroque altar of St James the Moor-Slayer in the parish church of **Santa María**. The latter church, Viana's most splendid monument, seems more like a cathedral than a parish church, and indeed was erroneously described as such by the 17th-century Italian pilgrim Laffi. Laffi was especially enthusiastic about Santa María's Renaissance south portal, which he praised for its 'most beautiful reliefs'. Designed in 1549 by Juan de Goyaz, a sculptor rather than an architect, it is a work of proto-baroque dynamism which looks ahead to Alonso Cano's 17th-century west façade of Granada cathedral. Like the latter work, it takes as its initial inspiration a Roman triumphal arch, but gives new life to this form, in this case by the bold insertion of an enormous coffered niche in the upper level; the lively carvings so admired by Laffi include a powerful Crucifixion group, various images of the Virgin, the mysteries of the Rosary, and some delightful classical grotesque work. The Gothic interior, much altered during the 16th century, is worthy of the portal, and its light and elegant character is much enhanced by traceried openings in the gallery; a final touch of splendour is lent by the baroque high altar of 1663–74, a gilded work of exquisite workmanship. The church, appropriately, was the burial place of the great Cesare Borgia, killed in a skirmish at Viana in 1507; his tomb, however, was later violated, and the only memorial to him is a modern bronze head outside the Town Hall.

Viana: the church of Santa María.

Viana: detail of the Renaissance south portal of Santa María.

THE RIOJA
LOGROÑO TO SANTO DOMINGO
DE LA CALZADA

West of Viana, the pilgrims' route descends into the wide and fertile valley of the Ebro, a valley famous for its wines and the excellence of its food. This is the heartland of La Rioja, a small and now autonomous region which at one time was much fought over by the kings of Navarre and Castile, all of them attracted by the land's strategical position and the wealth of its soil. The territory of Navarre extended at one time all the way to Nájera, but then in 1076 the troops of Alfonso VI pushed forward the Castillian frontier to Logroño, on the west bank of the Ebro. Aware of the importance of the Santiago pilgrimage to the whole development of the Rioja, Alfonso immediately set about improving the pilgrims' route through the region. The terrain is relatively flat, but it is crossed by several large rivers that provided formidable obstacles. Alfonso called on the services of St Dominic, who, together with his disciple and fellow monk, Juan de Quintanaortuño (later St John of Ortega), laid out paved stretches of road, founded hospitals, chapels and hostels, and constructed numerous bridges.

LOGROÑO

One of the most important of these new bridges was a 12-arched construction over the river Ebro at Logroño. Thanks to this bridge Logroño grew rapidly from a small farming community into a bustling pilgrimage centre, arranged, like Puente la Reina, alongside a long central street. The layout of medieval Logroño can still be appreciated, though few monuments of importance have survived from this early period, the town having been radically transformed in later centuries, when it developed as an important centre of agriculture and light industry. Today the capital of the Rioja, Logroño is a lively town of largely unprepossessing appearance, and is dominated by tall apartment and office blocks of the post-war years. Entering the town along the pilgrims' route, you cross the Ebro on the Puente de Piedra, a modern reconstruction of the bridge built by Sts Dominic and

(Opposite) Nájera: Santa María la Real — interior of the cloisters.

The pilgrims' way from Logroño to Santo Domingo de la Calzada.

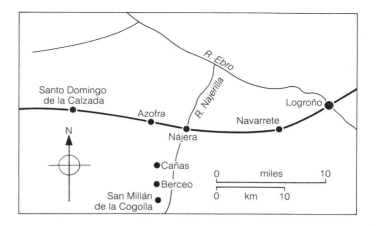

John of Ortega. Once across the river turn right on to the Rua Vieja, which, together with its continuation, the Calle Barriocepo, represented the main thoroughfare through medieval Logroño. These two streets still retain a picturesque medieval look, though the part of town in which they are situated has been shamefully neglected, and its old decaying buildings have now become the haunt of drug-addicts and other members of the town's marginal population. The first building which you come to on the Rua Vieja is the church of **Santa María de Palacio,** so called because it was built from the 13th century onwards over a Romanesque church attached to a palace of Alfonso VII. A small Romanesque door belonging to the original church remains, and leads into what is left of a 15th-century cloister. The rest of the building was heavily altered in between the 16th and 18th centuries, though it has kept a most interesting early 14th-century spire, which rises, unusually, not from a tower, but directly from the lantern of the church.

Deviating slightly from the pilgrims' route, and turning left at Santa María on to the Calle Palacio, you will come shortly to the Calle Herrerías, where you will find Logroño's oldest surviving monument. This, the church of **San Bartolomé,** has three Romanesque apses of the 12th century, a transitional Gothic nave, and an early 14th-century west façade richly carved in a stiff and rather archaic style with scenes from the life of St Bartholomew. Off the western end of the street is the former collegiate church which now serves as the town's **Cathedral**: the building was once attached to the order of the

Holy Sepulchre, and, like other buildings associated with this order, was octagonal in shape (hence its present name of Santa María de la Redonda, or St Mary of the Rotunda). Rebuilt from the 15th century onwards, the cathedral is mainly interesting for its magnificent and enormously tall west façade, begun in 1742 by Martín de Beratúa. The frontispiece of this façade, inspired probably by the south portal of Viana's parish church, takes the form of a gigantic coffered niche, the elaborate decoration of which forms a striking contrast to the

The Rua Vieja, the former pilgrims' route through Logroño.

A 17th-century representation of St James the Moor-Slayer above the south portal of the Church of Santiago, Logroño.

The 16th-century gateway at the end of the pilgrims' route through Logroño's old town.

entirely undecorated lower level of the twin towers which flank it; a further contrast is provided by the towers' complex and ornate upper levels. The singularly gloomy interior of the cathedral has late Gothic vaulting sprung from massive piers, the sobriety of the whole relieved only by the joyful Churrigueresque high altar and by the tracery in the arches of the aisles.

You can return to the Rua Vieja by way of the Calle Mercaderes, passing at No. 1306 a fine if extremely worn classical plateresque arch, attached to a crumbling 16th-century palace. The Rua Vieja ends in a small square adorned with a small pilgrims' fountain, dated 1655 but heavily and clumsily restored in recent times. The presence of this fountain is explained by the adjoining **Church of Santiago**, which was designed in the early 16th century by one Juan de Corella, and has a single-aisled late Gothic interior vaulted in a flamboyant style. Its 17th-century south portal looms over the pilgrims' fountain and is crowned by a massive and singularly dynamic representation of St James the Moor-Slayer, whose cult is particularly strong in the Rioja area, his bloody intervention in the famous battle against Abderraman II having taken place near the now ruined castle of Clavijo, only 15 km (9 miles) to the south of Logroño.

West of the church of Santiago, the pilgrims' route follows the Calle Barriocepo, passing the former **Convent of the Merced** (now a local government office), where you should stop briefly to see the charming 17th-century courtyard. Eventually you will come to the tiny remaining portion of Logroño's medieval walls, and leave the old town through an ogee-arched 16th-century gateway bearing the arms of Charles V. You are now faced with a rather dreary section of the pilgrims' route, and have to cross the extensive western suburbs of Logroño before entering a flat and prosperous countryside, criss-crossed with vines, orchards and wheatfields and much built over. The one place of interest before Nájera is **Navarrete**, a small village just off the N 111. Earlier in date than Logroño, and at one time the more important of the two settlements, it is now a modest place with some pleasant arcaded and cobbled streets. The large pilgrims' hostel which once stood here has been pulled down, but one of the hostel's 13th-century portals — a transitional Gothic work with vigorously carved geometrical motifs in the covings —

has been kept as the entrance to the cemetery on the western outskirts of the village.

Nájera, occupying a striking situation under sandstone cliffs formed by a bend in the river Najerilla, rose to fame during the rule of the kings of Navarre, who chose it as a royal residence and burial-place. The town continued to prosper after the annexation to Castile in 1076, benefiting greatly from the bridge built in the early 12th century by St John of Ortega; it was at the foot of this bridge, on the then unbuilt-up eastern banks of the river, that the saint established his first hermitage. At the end of the last century, the hermitage was demolished, and the old bridge replaced by a modern one; the town today has no important monument surviving from the early medieval period. The historic core of Nájera is a small and very attractive district squeezed in between the river and the sandstone cliffs to the west, and overshadowed by the massive bulk of the monastery of **Santa María la Real**. Just to the east of the latter is the parish church of **Santa Cruz**, originally a royal chapel attached to the monastery; the present building is a late 16th-century hall church, heavily restored in recent years, and with mainly baroque furnishings. Santa María la

NÁJERA

(Above) Detail of the tracery in the cloisters of Santa María la Real.

(Left) Nájera: cloisters of Santa María la Real.

Real stands directly under cliffs pockmarked with caves. Founded in 1054, it was made a dependency of the Abbey of Cluny in 1079, and then rebuilt after 1453. After being abandoned in 1835, it was put to a variety of uses, including barracks, warehouse, theatre and dance hall; restored at the end of the century, it has been occupied by Franciscan monks since 1895. The exterior of the church, distinguished by a series of giant cylindrical turrets, has a fortress-like severity, and is virtually undecorated save for the elegant Renaissance north portal through which you enter the building. The tall interior in pale ochre stone is remarkably simple for its late date, with quadripartite vaulting rather than the elaborate late Gothic vaulting that one might have expected; an unusual feature is the triforium, which runs around the eastern end of the church, and comprises plain and irregularly shaped openings that appear to have been cut directly out of the bare walls. A chapel off the south side of the church contains the superlatively carved 12th-century tomb of Queen Doña Blanca of Pamplona, while at the back of the church, under the choir, is a row of weathered tombs comprising the pantheon of the kings of Navarre. The most elaborate furnishings in the building are the walnut stalls of the upper choir, a fantastically intricate example of the 'Isabelline Gothic' style, executed in 1495 by the local artists Andrés and Nicolás Amutio. A doorway in the same style connects the church with the cloisters, the lower level of which, dating from the early 16th century, has Gothic arches adorned with tracery of lace-like elegance and complexity.

SAN MILLÁN
DE LA
COGOLLA

The stretch of the pilgrims' way in between Nájera and Santo Domingo de la Calzada is well worth doing on foot, departing as it does from the asphalted road, and passing through little spoilt countryside. To your right are extensive views over the plains of the Ebro Valley, while to your left rise the foothills of the Sierra de la Demanda. The southern half of the Rioja is wild and largely mountainous, and the further you move away from the Ebro Valley, the poorer the region becomes. From the friendly but ugly village of Azofra, 7 km (4 miles) west of Nájera on the pilgrims' route, a fascinating and unforgettably beautiful detour can be made to San Millán de la Cogolla, high up in these mountains, and much venerated by pilgrims to Santiago. On your way there from Azofra, you will pass the home village of St Dominic, **Cañas**, where there is an important Cistercian convent founded in 1170 and containing in its Gothic church one of Spain's most celebrated sepulchral monuments, the serenely elegant 14th-century tomb of Doña López de Haro. Shortly after Cañas, the road begins to climb, and you will soon reach the village of **Berceo**, the birthplace of Gonzalo de Berceo, the first poet in the Castillian language and a friend and contemporary of St Dominic.

San Millán de Cogolla lies just beyond, at the head of a lonely mountain valley, green and densely forested in its lower slopes, and bordered to the south by the peak of San Lorenzo, which is snow-capped for much of the year. It is a poor village, little spoilt by modern development, and with a narrow main street totally unsuitable for the increasing number of coach parties that come here at week-ends and in the summer months.

The fame of the place is due to the sixth-century hermit, St Millán, whose relics were among the most worshipped in Spain, and which attracted pilgrims almost immediately after the saint's death. There are two monasteries here named after him, the oldest and highest of the two, **San Millán de Suso**, marking the spot where the saint was born in 473, and where he died 101 years later. Occupying an isolated and most romantic forest setting high above the village, it is built against the side of a rock, into which has been hollowed out a Visigothic chapel containing the 12th-century sarcophagus of the saint, a work in dark-green alabaster featuring a memorable recumbent representation of him. The main body of the church was built between the ninth and tenth centuries and comprises two aisles separated by a long row of arches, Mozarabic and horseshoe-shaped at the east end, and Romanesque at the other. By the end of the 11th century, when the cult of St Millán was at its height, the upper monastery was abandoned, and its monks moved themselves and the precious relics of their saint down to a much larger foundation lower down the mountain. The lower monastery, known as **San Millán de Yuso**, was rebuilt between the 16th and 18th centuries, and towers over the surrounding village, for which reason it is sometimes refered to as the 'Escorial of the Rioja'.

The original Benedictine order moved out of the monastery in the last century, and the place fell into ruin. But it has recently been re-occupied by monks, who take visitors here on an interminably long guided tour. The main attraction is the treasury, with its 11th-century reliquary of St Millán, an exquisite ivory work carved with minute scenes from the life of the saint. The monastery itself, however, is in a depressing condition, badly neglected in parts, and over-restored in others. You enter through a heavy baroque frontispiece dominated by a relief of St James the Moor-Slayer; later you are taken into a cloister with elaborate late Gothic vaulting, but with a bare and gloomy character owing partly to its grey stone and partly to French troops having stripped it in the last century of much of its statuary. Eventually, you reach the church, a dark and cavernous Renaissance structure supported by a giant order of piers. The one cheerful moment in the whole complex comes in the 18th-century sacristy, a long white chamber adorned with gilded stucco and colourful rococo scrawls.

SANTO
DOMINGO DE
LA CALZADA

Continuing your walk west along the pilgrims' route from Azofra, your path passes shortly after leaving the village a medieval cross, an eloquent, solitary reminder of the early days of the pilgrimage. The landscape becomes greener and hillier until eventually, from the summit of one of the hills, you look down towards the distant town of Santo Domingo de la Calzada, which lies at the edge of the plains, stretched out by the eastern banks of the river Oja, and in the shadow of the soaring baroque tower of its cathedral. Known once as Burgo de Santo Domingo (the town of St Dominic), Santo Domingo de la Calzada was but an insignificant village until the late 11th century, when St Dominic had a 24-arched bridge built across the Oja. In the small hermitage which he put up alongside this the saint lived until his death in 1109, founding also in the vicinity a church, pilgrims' hostel and hospital, the latter surviving today as the state-run Parador. The church was built on a plot of land donated by Alfonso VI, who himself laid the first stone; in 1158 it was decided to replace this building with a large Collegiate church, which was to be accorded the status of cathedral in 1232, following the transference to the town of the bishop of Nájera. The town has continued to thrive over the centuries as an important agricultural centre, and has maintained as well a reputation for being one of the places on the *Camino Francés* most devoted to the Santiago pilgrimage.

The bustling modern town of Santo Domingo extends to the south of the N 111, but the pilgrims' route runs to the north of this road, taking you through a quiet area crammed with old buildings, one of which serves as the most luxuriously appointed pilgrims' refuge along the whole *Camino*. The dominant monument is the **Cathedral**, the bulk of which was completed by 1235. Its oldest section is the Romanesque apse, which has an exterior featuring fantastical heads in the corbels. The last addition was the magnificent baroque bell-tower, which was built in the 1760s to replace two earlier structures, including a medieval tower which had been struck by lightning. The present tower, the salient and most distinguished feature of the cathedral's exterior, was designed by the same architect responsible for the twin towers at Logroño cathedral,

Santo Domingo de la Calzada: detail of the south portal of the cathedral.

Martín de Beratúa, and is likewise characterized by an austere rectangular base, and an exuberant upper level, with an ornate octagonal drum supporting a tapering pile of ornamentation. The cathedral's south portal, through which you enter the building, is also by Martín de Beratúa, but is in a rather stiffer and more conventional style. The light and recently restored interior stuns through the wealth and variety of its detail. Most of the original fabric is in a transitional Gothic style, which accords well with the simplicity of the small Romanesque apse; the one elaborate feature of the architecture is the vaulting in the upper end of the church, which has rib-vaults suggestive perhaps of English influence. Against this relatively simple background is set a superlative range of late Gothic to Renaissance furnishings and decoration.

The main entrance lands you immediately in the south transept, where your attention is immediately drawn to the late Gothic tomb of St Dominic, a work of jewel-like intricacy executed in 1513 according to designs by the great Felipe Vigarny. While admiring this sculpture it is quite possible that you will be distracted by the sounds of a cock and a hen; turning round to the west wall of the transept, you will be confronted by what can unquestionably be described as the most splendid chicken coop in the world, and indeed the only one in a Renaissance plateresque style. This curious feature, the town's greatest claim to fame, owes its existence to a posthumous miracle of St Dominic whereby the crowing of a roasted cock and hen attested to the innocence of a wrongly executed pilgrim; descendants of these supernatural animals have been kept in the church ever since, and people still proudly collect their feathers. A further excellent example of Renaissance plateresque workmanship, though without kinetic additions, is the decoration surrounding the chapel just to the west of this transept. Meanwhile, in the centre of the nave, is a Renaissance choir, containing elaborate wooden stalls of 1521, and decorated on the outside with beautifully fresh and colourful scenes of the life of St Dominic. Also of note is the second chapel on the left of the nave (the chapel of the Magdalena) which, too, has finely executed plateresque decoration, but in an Isabelline Gothic style. Finally, mention should be made of the gilded and towering high altar, the last work of Damian Forment, who died in 1540, while still

Santo Domingo de la Calzada cathedral: chamber opening on the west wall of the south transept containing a live hen and cock.

engaged on it; Forment's long career embraces the Gothic and Renaissance styles, and in this exceptionally dynamic work he reveals himself to be a worthy rival to the Spanish follower of Michelangelo, Alonso de Berruguete.

The much-altered former pilgrims' hospital, now the Parador, faces the south side of the cathedral, while on the other side of the cathedral is a large and pleasant square bordered to the north by the Renaissance **Town Hall**, a long arcaded building, balconied in its upper level, and with a rich frontispiece bearing the arms of Charles V. The most sophisticated of the town's 16th-century buildings is the **Convent of St Francis**, in the western end of town. It was erected in 1571 according to designs supplied by Juan de Herrera, the favourite architect of Philip II. Fray Bernardo de Fresneda, confessor to the king, lies prominently buried in the crossing of the convent's church, a building in the shape of a Latin cross and with the perfect proportions and cold geometrical regularity associated with the Herrera style. From the convent it is a short walk down to the river and to St Dominic's impressive **Bridge**. The next stretch of the pilgrims' route is along the N 111, which after 7 km (4 miles) crosses into the province of Burgos.

OLD CASTILE
REDECILLA TO CARRIÓN DE LOS CONDES

Once into the province of Burgos you enter the large and recently formed Castilla y León, an administrative entity comprising the former kingdom of León and most of the region known as Old Castile. The name Castile dates back to at least 801 and refers to the countless castles that were erected here as successive bulwarks in the fight against Islam. The original region, occupying the upper Ebro Valley, became in the early eighth century a 'County' or petty sovereignty subject at first to the kings of León. In the course of fighting back the Moors, its territory began rapidly to expand, and by the tenth century, its growing independence had become a subject of much concern to the long-established kingdoms of León and Asturias; the most famous of its rulers during this period was Fernán González, who by the uniting of various fiefdoms managed to extend what he fancifully called his 'kingdom' all the way from Santander in the north to the Duero in the south. Officially Castile was only made a Kingdom in 1035, its first king, Ferdinand I, becoming later sovereign of León following his marriage with Sancha, daughter and heiress of Bermudo III. Subsequently the two kingdoms were separated, but they were rejoined again in the 13th century under St Ferdinand; in 1474 they were inherited by Isabel la Católica, whose marriage five years earlier to Ferdinand of Aragon had finally paved the way for a united Spain. Long before this happened, the pushing back of the Moorish frontier further and further to the south had led to a distinction being made between the northern and southern halves of Castile, the former coming to be known as 'old' the latter as 'the new'.

Castile is often thought of as the heartland of Spain, not only because of its central and dominating position, but also because its early counts and kings were the first to make an organized stand against the Moors. Furthermore the people and landscapes of this region have been seen by many as representing the 'quintessential Spain'. The hackneyed image of the Spaniards as a proud, melancholy and mystical race,

(Opposite) Burgos cathedral from the east, featuring in the foreground the plateresque Capilla del Condestable.

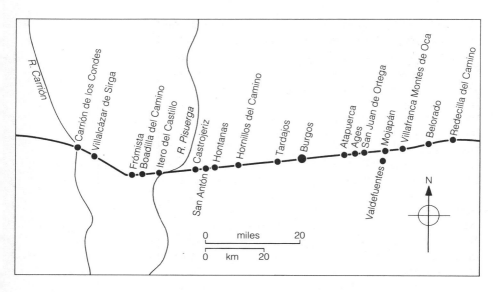

The pilgrims' way from Redecilla del Camino to Carrión del los Condes.

obsessed by death and visions of past grandeur, has its roots in Castile, and is based to a large extent on an interpretation of the extraordinary Castillian landscape, which is quite unlike any other in Europe. At its most characteristic it is a land of endless plateaux, scorched by the sun, blown by the wind, framed by distant glimpses of gaunt mountains, and interspersed with rocky outcrops and solitary lines of poplars. After Burgos the pilgrim faces what is in many ways the cruellest stretch of the pilgrims' way, a scene of often numbing monotony conducive to introspection. Yet it should also be said that for the architectural traveller it is above all in Castile that the original, idiosyncratic features of Spanish architecture first become fully apparent.

REDECILLA
DEL CAMINO,
BELORADO
AND
VILLAFRANCA
MONTES DE
OCA

After crossing into the province of Burgos, the pilgrims' route continues to follow the N 120, which from this point on offers excellent views over meadows and wheat-fields of the distant and often snow-capped range of the Sierra de la Demanda. You pass through a series of small villages, the first of which, Redecilla del Camino, is also one of the prettiest and best preserved, its simple houses with projecting upper floors and wooden eaves lining a long main street; in its rustic baroque church of the **Virgen de la Calle** is to be found, incongruously, an outstanding 12th-century baptismal font, carved with what appears to be a representation of a celestial city. Belorado, the first sizeable community after Santo Domingo de la Calzada, dates back to Roman times, and has a number of medieval and later monuments, most notably the 16th-century church of **Santa María**, which has a light and very wide interior featuring massive cylindrical piers from which the ribs of the late Gothic vaults spring in tree-like fashion. Eleven km (7 miles) further on is the village of Villafranca Montes de Oca, the half-way point between Santo Domingo and Burgos, and a major stop on the pilgrims' way. This small, semi-abandoned, and slightly hostile place was once the important Visigothic settlement of Auca, and the seat of a bishopric which was later transferred to Burgos. It stands at the edge of the Montes de Oca, a forested mountainous region which, historically, marks the true frontier of Castile.

At Villafranca, the pilgrims' route departs from the main road and climbs up into the mountains, passing, on the upper outskirts of the village, the ruins of the large pilgrims' **Hospital of San Antón**; founded in the 14th century, and now undergoing extensive reconstruction, it has a simple 16th-century gate and a balconied courtyard dating back to the 15th century. A steepish path leads you through trees and meadows up to the spring of **Mojapán** a shaded, idyllic spot enjoying a magnificent panorama over forests to distant peaks. To the pilgrims who once came here, however, the pleasures of the place must have been balanced by a knowledge of the dangers of the densely forested stretch to come. Notorious for its robbers, this was also an area where numerous pilgrims got lost, including Laffi, who had to survive for a while on wild mushrooms. Today the route offers no such excitements, and shortly beyond Mojapán enters a long fire-break offering frequent glimpses of the nearby main road. You can make a short detour down to the road to see the remains of **Valdefuentes**, a Cistercian priory and hospital founded in the 12th century. All that remains is the heavily constructed apse, now turned into a roadside chapel facing a picnic area littered with rubbish; on one of the chapel walls are some incongruous lines of the medieval poet Gonzalo de Berceo recording the consoling peace and beauty of the verdant site.

SAN JUAN DE ORTEGA

Whereas it is difficult today to imagine Valdefuentes as a welcome scene for the tired pilgrim, the arrival at San Juan de Ortega is one of the highpoints of the whole route. After wandering endlessly through forest, you come suddenly to a clearing in which is huddled a small group of apparently abandoned buildings. In this hamlet, several kilometres from the main road, only a handful of people remain today, one of whom, Don José María Alonso, is the priest in sole charge of the ruined hermitage founded by St John of Ortega in around 1142, and lived in by Jeronymite monks from 1431 up to the place's dissolution in 1835. Like St John of Ortega and his followers, José María Alonso is dedicated to the well-being of passing pilgrims, to whom he offers food as well as accommodation in dormitories around a small 15th-century cloister with depressed arches in the lower gallery.

The history of San Juan de Ortega goes back to a pilgrims' refuge, put up by St John on the edge of this once inhospitable area. Later on the saint went on a journey to the Holy Land, and on his return had been caught up in a storm at sea from which he had been saved by the miraculous intercession of St Nicholas of Bari. He decided to settle in the Montes de Oca, and to build here a chapel dedicated to the saint who had saved

San Juan de Ortega: the west façade of the former monastery church, and, to the left, the chapel built by Isabel la Católica to house the mausoleum of St John of Ortega.

San Juan de Ortega: the apse of the former monastery church designed by St John himself.

him. He was buried in the chapel on his death in 1163, and three centuries later his tomb was covered by a superb **Mausoleum**. Shortly after the mausoleum's construction, it was visited by Isabel la Católica, who later claimed that the experience had cured her of her infertility. She had the **Chapel** completely rebuilt, thinking that the mausoleum required a more worthy setting than the simple Romanesque structure which had been designed by the saint himself. The new structure stands at the eastern end of the row of ruinous buildings which contains the priest's house and leads to the monastery church. Its severe western façade is of the late 16th century, and comprises a large arch in which has recently been placed a magnificent Renaissance grille taken from the chancel of the adjacent church; the interior, divided in two by another grille, has dainty late Gothic vaulting with bosses bearing the coat of arms of Isabel and her husband Ferdinand.

As for the mausoleum, this was moved in 1966 to the crossing of the **Monastery Church**, a beautiful building in the form of a Greek cross, begun by St John of Ortega following his work on the chapel. The three apses and part of the crossing were completed by the saint and reveal him to be a considerable architect. Especially fine is the central apse, which features an elegant arrangement of two superimposed rows of blind arcading on the exterior, and, inside, three openings with receding arches creating an effect of great depth. Among the sculpted Romanesque capitals in the crossing is a superlative

The Isabelline plateresque mausoleum of St John of Ortega.

Annunciation, popularly famed for a peculiar light effect (known as the 'miracle of light') which can be observed each equinox: on these occasions (21 March and 22 September), at exactly 5 pm solar time, a solitary ray of sun strikes the virgin's belly. Work was abandoned on the church after St John's death, and was not taken up again until the early 15th century, when the building was completed in a simple Gothic style. The mausoleum, now in the crossing and surrounded by exquisite plateresque iron work, is attributed by some to the great Gil de Siloe; it is at any rate an excellent example of the light and fanciful Isabelline Gothic style, and contains around its base charming scenes of the life of St John. A door in the crossing leads into the large, late 17th-century extension to the monastery, centred around an austere and monumental cloister now in a deplorable condition.

AGES

The narrow and picturesque tree-lined lane in front of the church heads off in the direction of Burgos. Those on foot climb over a gentle hill to the tiny, unspoilt village of Ages, where there is a one-arched **Bridge** by St John of Ortega, standing in isolation among fields. At Atapuerca, the following village, you ascend a further and steeper ridge and soon catch your first glimpse of the vast fertile plateau in which Burgos is situated. The approach to Burgos from the east is especially unattractive, and you would be well advised to avoid the city's extensive eastern suburbs and take a bus from the outlying village of Villafría directly into the city centre.

BURGOS

Burgos, a city notorious for its biting winds and climatic extremes, has its origins in a fortress founded in 884 on the bank of the Arlanzón. In the mid-10th century Fernán González made it capital of what was later to become the kingdom of Castile, and as such it emerged as the leading Christian town of Spain, the main centre of the so-called Reconquest, and a place of vital importance in the history of the Santiago pilgrimage. In 1087, the Castillian court was transferred from Burgos to the recently captured Toledo, and thereafter began a great dispute over which city deserved precedence, a dispute which was not finally to be resolved until

1492, with the creation of Valldolid as capital of Spain. Though Burgos' political importance had diminished by the end of the 15th century, its economic life prospered as never before, thanks to the city's domination of the wool trade. Decline only set in at the beginning of the 17th century, as a result of a series of plagues, a collapse in the wool market, and the economic recession which had begun to affect Spain generally at this period. There has been a renewal of prosperity since the early 19th century, but the city has never regained its former vitality. Deeply conservative, and briefly the Nationalist capital during the Spanish Civil War, Burgos remains today heavily under the stultifying influence of the Church and Army. Fortunately, in compensation, Burgos is also a university city, and at night the streets around the cathedral become the centre of great student animation. Furthermore the inherent conservatism of Burgos has had its positive side as well, namely in the way in which the town centre has been spared to a remarkable extent from offending modern development.

To the tourist the attraction of Burgos lies essentially in its cathedral, but there are also numerous other monuments that merit a visit: indeed there is perhaps more to see in Burgos than in any other town along the pilgrims' way. Entering the city from the east, the first monuments that await you are around the Plaza San Juan Lesmes, on the eastern bank of a tiny tributary of the Arlanzón, just outside the former city walls. On the eastern side of this square are the remains of the large Benedictine **Monastery of San Juan** of the late 15th and early 16th centuries, part of which now houses a **Museum** to the 19th-century local painter Marceliano Santa María; it comprises an attractive cloister combining Gothic vaulting and classical arcading. Belonging to this monastery was one of the more than thirty pilgrims' hospitals that were established in Burgos by the late 15th century, none of which survive in good condition; of this particular hospital only the late Gothic main portal remains, attached to a hideous Fascist building of the 1950s, now functioning as a Casa de Cultura. Facing this portal, on the northern side of the square, is a church dedicated to the patron saint of Burgos, **San Juan Lesmes**, a French abbot who was invited by Alfonso VI to come to Spain to help replace the Mozarabic liturgy with the Roman one, and who

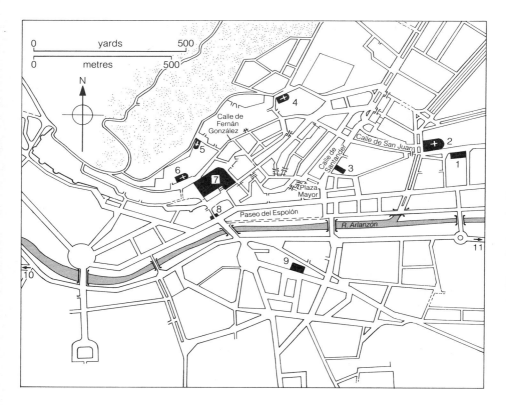

ended his days in Burgos, caring for pilgrims. The Romanesque church built in his memory in 1074 was pulled down at the end of the 14th century and replaced by another structure, in turn restored and remodelled in the early 16th century, and again in more recent times. Its richly decorated late Gothic main entrance, on the southern side, is the most distinguished feature of an otherwise plain exterior; the interior, meanwhile, is notable essentially for its elaborate vaulting, and its late Gothic to baroque tombs and furnishings, including a superlative Renaissance pulpit with medallions and acanthus decoration.

Crossing the small bridge to the west of the church, you go through the medieval San Juan Gate, and enter the well preserved old town, the pilgrims' route through which is followed by the narrow Calle de San Juan and its continuation, the Calle de Fernán González. At the first crossing, the

Calle de Santander, you should make a brief detour to the left to see the **Casa del Cordón**, one of the finest of the city's palaces. Built in the late 15th century for Don Pedro Fernández de Velasco, the Constable or Condestable of Castile, its architect was probably Simón de Colonia, from whom Don Pedro had commissioned the famous Capilla del Condestable in the cathedral. Its main façade overlooks the quiet Plaza del Mercado Mayor — at one time the lively nucleus of Burgos life — and features a main portal surrounded by a realistically carved knotted cord (the Franciscan motif), a typical example of the plateresque use of heraldic motifs as a major element in the decoration of a building.

Just beyond the point where the Calle de San Juan turns into the Calle de Fernán González, a flight of steps to the right leads up to the church of **San Gil**, a late 14th-century structure altered at the end of the following century and with later additions. The tall west façade is virtually undecorated, and the nave and crossing are similarly austere, with simple quadripartite vaulting. The late 15th-century chancel has vaulting of a more complex type, and with richly carved bosses; but nothing prepares you for the early 16th-century **Capilla de la Navidad**, which is inspired by the Capilla del Condestable, and has a magnificent star-shaped vault centred on a roundel pierced with openings. Further north along the Calle de Fernán González, another uphill turning to your right will take you to the church of **San Esteban**, which is built directly underneath the ruined citadel of Burgos. Dating back to the late 13th century, this church too underwent numerous modifications after the late 15th century. Its west façade, featuring a large rosette window rebuilt in 1479, still retains its original portal. Similar to those in the cathedral's cloister, it has a lintel in the form of a depressed arch supporting a tympanum divided into two layers of sculptural decoration: the upper layer is of Christ in Judgement flanked by the Virgin and St John, and the lower one is of the Martyrdom of St Stephen. The wide and light interior combines Gothic and Renaissance features, and has an early 16th century upper choir by Simón de Colonia, as well as a number of fine Renaissance tombs. Returning to the Calle Fernan González, it is now only a short walk to the cathedral, which was once entered by pilgrims from the north portal. Today you have to walk down a large flight of steps, and enter the building either from the west or south. Before making the descent you should visit the church of **San Nicolás**, which occupies a commanding position directly in front of the cathedral's west façade. This is a 15th-century building richly endowed by a wealthy mercantile family, one of whose members, Gonzalo Polanco, commissioned in around 1500 the staggeringly ornate high altar, which takes up the entire east end of the church, and runs from the floor right up to the ceiling. Carved in stone by Francisco de Colonia to designs supplied by his father, Simón, it is a Gothic plateresque work of an intricacy to be found in Burgos only in the Charterhouse and in the later parts of the cathedral.

BURGOS
CATHEDRAL

The **Cathedral**, one of the largest and richest in Spain, provides a fascinating insight into the development of Spanish architecture, and shows the way in which French and German influences were transformed into an unmistakeably Spanish style. The first stones of the present building were laid in 1221 by Ferdinand III and Bishop Maurice, the latter a man of probably English origin who had spent a long period in France. The name of the architect is not known, but it is generally assumed that he was a Frenchman brought to Spain by Bishop Maurice on his return from Paris; if not French, he was certainly someone with considerable knowledge of French architecture. At any rate the building was put up at considerable speed and was largely complete by the middle of the 13th century with the exception of the central lantern tower, and the upper stages of the twin towers of the west façade. The next major building phase was begun in the late 15th century and was directed by a family of German origin headed by Juan de Colonia (John of Cologne), and including his son, Simón, and grandson, Francisco; the lantern tower, built by them, was reconstructed in the mid-16th century by one Juan de Vallejo. The Colonias and their followers gave to the cathedral its fantastically pinnacled and crotchetted look, and also greatly contributed to the overall decorative profusion which in many ways is the hallmark of Spain's architectural genius. Yet their additions have often been criticized by the more puritanically-minded for concealing the supposed purity of the original structure. Thus G.E. Street, while recognizing that from afar

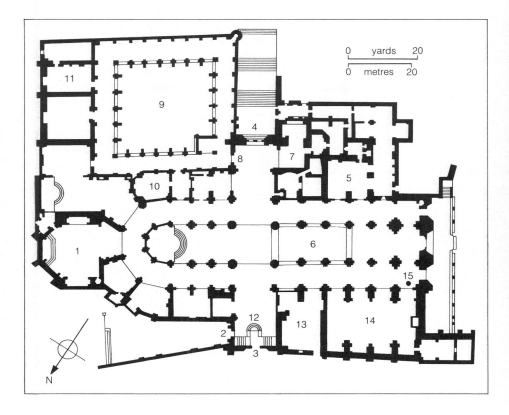

0 yards 20
0 metres 20

these accretions create an effect of picturesque richness, wrote of the cathedral that 'Never was a church more altered for the worse after its first erection than was this.'

To appreciate the complex evolution of Burgos cathedral, it is best not to go immediately inside the building but to spend some time looking at the **Exterior**. Already, approaching it along the Calle de Fernán González, you will have had the best view of the east end and crossing, and appreciated the building's sloping site. The easternmost part is made up of the enormous **Capilla del Condestable**, decorated in a florid Gothic style and crowned by a pinnacled octagon, the shape of which is echoed in the even more complex tower of the crossing. G.E. Street was delighted to find that behind all the pinnacles, crockets and other decorative embellishments that dominate the vista there had survived far more of the original structure than he had

Burgos Cathedral
1. Capilla del Condestable
2. Puerta de la Pellerjería 3. Puerta de la Coronería
4. Puerta del Sarmental
5. Capilla de la Presentación
6. Choir 7. Capilla de la Visitación
8. Cloister portal
9. Cloister 10. Sacristy
11. Museum 12. Escalera Dorada 13. Capilla de Santa Ana
14. Capilla de San Tecla 15. Clock (Papamoscas)

North transept portal by Francisco de Colonia, with scenes of the martyrdom of St John the Baptist and St John the Evangelist.

The Puerta del Sarmental with tympanum of Christ and the Four Evangelists.

previously imagined. The buttressed apse to which the Capilla del Condestable clings like some bloated, fantastical mollusc is in fact little changed from the outside, as are the two transepts. Streets' particular enthusiasm was reserved for the latter, the façades of which he described as being 'as fine as those of the best of our French or English churches.' The two façades are closely similar, and consist of a sculpted portal, a rose window, and an upper traceried gallery lined with statues and flanked by turrets, an arrangement possibly inspired by the transept façades of Rheims cathedral. The Calle de Fernán González passes right alongside the north portal, which is on a higher level to the north transept's eastern entrance (**Puerta de la Pellejería**), a classical plateresque work by Francisco de Colonia and containing reliefs of the martyrdom of John the Baptist and John the Evangelist. The sculptures on both the north and south portals are lively, naturalistic works of the mid-13th century, and are perhaps the finest of the cathedral's surviving early medieval sculptures. The north portal, known as the **Puerta de la Coronería**, is flanked by near life-sized representations of the twelve Apostles, and has a tympanum representing the Blessed and the Damned on its lower level, and Christ in Judgement on the upper one; the south portal, or **Puerta del Sarmental**, which rises up on steps, has a tympanum especially notable for its four, agitated Evangelists balanced around a majestic seated Christ. Sadly, the cathedral's imposing west façade has lost its three portals, the whole structure having been radically altered, not by the Colonias, but in the late 18th century. The lower half of this façade has today a flat and lifeless character, and the structure only begins to excite in its upper stages. The main survival of the 13th-century façade is the elegant traceried gallery which runs above the rebuilt rose window and has statues of Spanish kings between its columns. Above this is an elaborate balustrade marking the beginning of Juan de Colonia's contribution and emblazoned with the large Gothic lettering so typical of the Spanish plateresque. The openwork spires that crown the two flanking towers were not completed until the 19th century, but the design was Colonia's and clearly influenced by contemporary German cathedrals, such as that of his native Cologne.

Numerous comparisons have been made between the **Interior of Burgos Cathedral** and that of French Gothic buildings, most notably Bourges cathedral, which has a similar ground-plan. The overall effect, however, is unmistakeably Spanish, and not only on account of the centrally placed choir which impedes a clear view down the nave. The triforium, described by Street as 'being more curious than beautiful' and certainly 'from the hand of a native artist', has semi-circular arches similar to those in Bourges, but pierced by unusual and irregular openings, and ringed with amusing portrait heads such as would not be found in the great Gothic cathedrals of France. More importantly there is virtually no space between either the main arcade and the triforium, or between the triforium and the clerestory; the resulting proportions thus lack the soaring quality of the French high Gothic, and have instead a characteristically Spanish heaviness.

As with so many Spanish churches, the pleasure of a visit to Burgos cathedral owes much to the wealth of decoration and sculpture to be seen within. Touring the interior in an anti-clockwise direction, you can begin with the first chapel to the right of the nave, which contains the cathedral's most venerated image, a 14th-century statue of Christ, covered in leather which is popularly thought to be human skin, and with a beard and hair which are definitely of human origin. Of greater artistic and architectural interest is the adjoining **Capilla de la Presentación**, a spacious early 16th-century structure with star vaulting and a Renaissance alabaster tomb of Don Gonzalo de Lerma by Felipe de Vigarny. Opposite the chapel, in the very centre of the nave, is the **Choir**, which was moved here in the early 16th century in accordance with plans put forward by Vigarny, a decision which was the cause of much controversy. Vigarny, in collaboration with lesser artists, executed after 1505 the elegant wooden stalls, but the exterior casing of the choir is uninspired 17th-century work. Tall baroque grilles link the choir with the presbytery, where there is a profusely gilded high altar of the late 16th century. One's attention should be directed on this altar, and yet as soon as one nears the centre of the cathedral, it is difficult not to be distracted by the crossing and its extraordinary lantern. Large and ornate cylindrical piers — inevitably criticized by Street for being ungainly — support trumpet squinches that for once live up to their name and announce with a jubilant fanfair the brilliant, ornament-encrusted octagon above, the centrepiece of which is a radiant

star so pierced by openings that it appears to hover in the air; appropriately the lantern now serves as a canopy for the tomb of Burgos' best known hero, 'El Cid', whose tomb — marked by a simple slab — was transferred to the centre of the crossing in 1921.

Enthralling though this lantern is, the cathedral has numerous other surprises and treasures in store for you, beginning with the south transept, off whose south-western corner is the **Capilla de la Visitación**, an early work by Juan de Colonia, who lies buried near its entrance; of its various tombs, the most notable is that of Don Alonso de Cartagena, executed between 1490–5 by Gil de Siloe, whose late Gothic sculptures are among the greatest achievements of the Burgos school. Facing this chapel, on the other side of the transept, is the magnificent **Cloister Portal**, a French-style work of the 13th century, with a tympanum of the Baptism of Christ, and large, flanking figures representing the Annunciation and David and Isaiah. The serene and leisurely style of these sculptures contrast with the lively, busy panels of filigree workmanship to be found on the doors themselves: they portray the Descent into Limbo and Christ Riding into Jerusalem, and are by an unknown artist of the later 15th century whom many have liked to identify with Gil de Siloe. The **Cloister** today is entered from the ambulatory, through a door near that of the late 18th-century **Sacristy**, a light and cheerful rococo structure which was much derided by the Spanish neoclassical critic Antonio Ponz, and is generally and unfairly ignored by most visitors to the cathedral. In contrast the cloister has met with most people's approval, being an untouched work of the late 13th and early 14th centuries, featuring two superimposed Gothic arcades, and numerous fine tombs. The cathedral **Museum** which lies off it is popularly known for its chest which supposedly belonged to El Cid, and for its even more questionable painting by Leonardo da Vinci, one of many dubiously attributed works that hang in this dingy space; the main interest is the powerfully expressive statue of the Flagellated Christ by Gil de Siloe's son, Diego, whose masterpiece in the cathedral still awaits you.

Continuing to walk around the ambulatory you should pay particular attention to the altar screen, which has five outstanding marble reliefs by Felipe Vigarny, works

(Opposite) Interior of Burgos cathedral.

combining late Gothic animation and crowded compositions with a plethora of Renaissance detail. Finally you should enter the Capilla del Condestable, a soaring octagonal space built as the burial chapel of Pedro Fernández de Velasco and his wife Mencía de Mendoz. Designed by Simón de Colonia, but completed by his son Francisco, it is one of the highpoints of the Isabelline Gothic Style, with a most intricately ornamented lower level (featuring the prominent heraldic motifs so characteristic of the plateresque period) bursting into a colourful lantern ringed with stained glass windows and vaulted in stellar fashion, the central star transformed by openings into a work of lace-like delicacy: the upper level was clearly the main inspiration behind the later tower in the crossing. The rich appearance of the chapel is greatly enhanced by its furnishings, which include two polychromed altars by Vigarny and Diego de Siloe, and another altar by Gil de Siloe executed in collaboration with his son Diego.

It was in his capacity as an architect rather than as a sculptor that the versatile Diego de Siloe produced his most important work in Burgos. This, the **Escalera Dorada** or Golden staircase, was commissioned for the north transept in 1519 by Bishop Rodríguez de Fonseca, who was anxious to placate those who had criticized his earlier decision to close up completely the cathedral's north portal, and to allow outside access into the transept solely through Francisco de Colonia's lower door. Siloe's staircase was intended as an elegant and practical replacement to the small and frequently congested flight of steps which had originally led from the north portal down into the cathedral. One of the earliest examples of the introduction of Italian Renaissance ideas into Spain, it takes as its initial inspiration Bramante's staircase in the Vatican Belvedere, and has a central single flight of steps dividing into two on the first landing: this solution was shortly afterwards to be adopted by Michelangelo in his Laurentian Library in Florence. What makes Siloe's work so distinctively Spanish is the wealth of ornamentation, not only in the stonework itself, but also in the exquisitely wrought and gilded bronze railings; it is one of the Spanish classical works most truly deserving the name 'plateresque'.

Leaving the transept and turning right down the northern aisle of the nave, you will find a good example of the earlier

'Gothic' plateresque style in an exceptionally elaborate polychromed altar by Gil de Siloe, kept in the first chapel on the right, the **Capilla de Santa Ana**. The next and largest chapel of the nave is the virtually unvisited **Capilla de San Tecla**, built between 1731 and 1736 in a Churrigueresque style, covered in swirling blue and red stucco, and dominated by an altar of gilded salamonicas (twisted columns): coming to this chapel after having toured the rest of the cathedral makes one fully appreciate the extent to which the Spanish baroque has its roots in the plateresque. Before leaving the cathedral you should take a look up at the famous and very popular 14th-century **Clock** which is placed in the clerestory of the nave's westernmost bay, and stars the grotesque colourful figure of *Papamoscas* or 'the Fly-Squatter', whose gesture in killing the flies strikes the clock's bell.

From the cathedral the pilgrims' route continues west along the Calle Fernán González, eventually to leave the old town through the medieval St Martin's gate and cross the Arlanzón by the Malatos bridge, which brings you near to the monastery of Las Huelgas Reales. However to see more of medieval Burgos you should head south from the cathedral and cross the river at a much lower point. In between the cathedral and the river is the **Puerta de Santa María**, which was originally commissioned in 1536 as a free-standing triumphal arch, but was later executed as a replacement to one of the town's medieval gates. Designed by Francisco de Colonia and Juan de Vallejo, it is an imposing battlemented structure with a Renaissance frontispiece displaying statues of Charles V and such Burgos heroes as Fernán González and El Cid. East of the gate runs the riverside Paseo del Espolón, a promenade shaded by the grafted branches of parallel rows of curiously bollarded oaks, a common feature of the towns in this part of Castile. The Paseo ends near a modern statue of a ludicrously hirsute El Cid, in front of which is the Puente San Pablo. By the late middle ages Burgos had expanded on to the northern banks of the Arlanzón, and if you cross the river at this point you will find, amidst much ugly modern development, a number of fine old buildings.

The greatest of the palaces here, indeed one of the

OTHER BUILDINGS IN BURGOS

Puerta de Santa
María, Burgos.

Renaissance jewels of the city, is the **Casa de Miranda**, which was built in 1545, and has extensive classical grotesque decoration on its southern façade (on the Calle de Miranda), as well as in its delightful courtyard; today the building houses the city's archaeological and fine arts museum. Before heading west from here and regaining the pilgrims' route at Las Huelgas Reales, you should visit the Charterhouse or Cartuja, which lies 3 km (2 miles) east of the museum, and can be reached by bus from the adjoining bus station.

CARTUJA DE
MIRAFLORES

Enjoying a wooded, hill-top situation outside the town, the **Cartuja de Miraflores** is one of the high points of a tour of Burgos and a place which brings together all the great names associated with the city's cultural life in the 15th century. The grounds on which it was built were once the hunting grounds of John II, who handed them over to the Carthusian order in 1441; the property is still owned by the Carthusians, and the only place which they still own in Spain where visitors are allowed. The monastery church, begun in 1454 by Juan de Colonia and completed by his son Simón 30 years later, stands on the eastern side of a small and rather sombre cloister, and was built as the burial chapel of John II and his queen, Isabel of Portugal. A flamboyant Gothic west portal displaying two prominent coats of arms leads into a long, single-aisled structure with elaborate vaulting bearing further heraldic motifs in the bosses. The polygonal chancel, reached through a sequence of clearly segregated spaces (a typical feature of a Carthusian church, and a way of dividing the monks from the laity) is slightly wider than the nave and has crocketed ribs in the ceiling, as well as Flemish stained glass windows of the late 15th century. But what makes this chancel so remarkable is the sculptural decoration by Gil de Siloe, comprising the polychromed high altar, the star-shaped tomb of John and Isabel below this, and the flanking tomb of prince Don Alfonso on the north wall. These are all works of endlessly fascinating complexity, and of an intricacy which has rarely been equalled.

Whereas the Charterhouse is relatively little visited, the **Convent of Las Huelgas Reales**, on the western outskirts of the city, attracts almost as many crowds as the cathedral. Occupying a large walled area in what is today a green and wealthy suburb of Burgos, it is a Cistercian institution standing over what was once a summer residence belonging to the kings of Castile (the word *huelga* means 'repose'). Founded in 1187 by Alfonso VII at the request of his wife Eleanor (daughter of Henry II of England), it was intended for nuns of royal or aristocratic lineage, and served also as a royal pantheon, and as a place where numerous Spanish kings were knighted before God, a ceremony instituted by Ferdinand III in 1219. The attraction of the convent to so many Spanish visitors lies essentially in its historical associations, which are indeed more interesting than either the architecture or the furnishings. Architecturally it is a mess, with fascinating parts adding up to a rather unsatisfactory and over-restored whole. The church, built between *c.* 1180 and 1230, is in a simple Gothic style and was by an architect of either English or Angevin origin. Its chancel is largely taken up by a gilded

LAS HUELGAS
REALES

baroque high altar, while the nave is cut off by a wall from the rest of the church, and functions as a nuns' choir, complete with Renaissance stalls. An intricate Mudéjar door takes you through into a large 13th-century cloister, which has Gothic vaulting containing sections of recently uncovered Mudéjar workmanship; a room off its west side has a beautiful and important collection of early textiles. A smaller and largely rebuilt Romanesque cloister follows, off which is an intriguing Mudéjar chapel of *c.* 1200. Finally, in a corner of the adjoining gardens, is the delightful **Chapel of Santiago**, a small Mudéjar brick structure entered through a horseshoe arch: inside is an *artesonado* ceiling and an unusual 13th-century statue of the enthroned St James, whose outstretched hand holding a sword was constructed so as to move, thus enabling Ferdinand III to be knighted by someone who was not an inferior.

(Above) The Mudéjar chapel of Santiago, Convent of Las Huelgas Reales.

(Opposite) The gate to the Convent of Las Huelgas Reales.

A walk across unkempt parkland shaded by large trees takes you from Las Huelgas to the Burgos monument most eloquent of the Santiago pilgrimage. This, the **Hospital del Rey**, was founded as a pilgrims' hospital by Alfonso VIII in 1195, and functioned as such up to 1835, when it was badly damaged by fire; the buildings further suffered when used as a barracks during the Civil War, and today the place is undergoing extensive rebuilding prior to being used as the law faculty of Burgos University. Most of what you see today dates from the Renaissance and baroque periods, beginning with the early 16th-century entrance gate, which is crowned by classical plateresque decoration incorporating the pilgrim's scallop. The hospital church, to the left of the small courtyard on the other side of the gate, has a portico covered with further Renaissance ornamentation, this time featuring both the scallop motif and a representation of Santiago Matamoros. The tower which rises above this is baroque, as is the nave of the church, but the west portal is a solitary survival of the original early Gothic structure. The portal is known as the **Puerta de Romeros** or 'Pilgrims' Portal', and has magnificent Renaissance doors with ornate wooden panels, one of which shows a group of pilgrims.

After Burgos, the pilgrims' route departs completely from the main road, and follows a succession of side-roads almost all

BEYOND
BURGOS

The pilgrims' route
through Hornillos del
Camino.

The pilgrims' route
through Hornillos del
Camino.

the way to León; large stretches of the original unasphalted road survive, starting off with a near uninterrupted track between Burgos and Frómista. For those walking the route, the feeling of leaving the 20th century becomes greater than ever before, though, on the negative side, the landscape is progressively flatter and bleaker, and while you might find it at first to be hauntingly evocative, it ends by wearying both the feet and spirit. One of the first villages which you come to is **Hornillos del Camino**, little more than a long, wide and half-deserted main street, lined with simple, heavily built stone buildings, but with no trace left of the pilgrims' hospitals that were once here. A couple of abandoned communities come next, followed, after the village of Hontanas, by among the most impressive ruins along the whole *Camino*, those of the former monastery and hospital of **San Antón**. Founded in the 12th century to care for those suffering from St Anthony's fire (a form of leprosy), it has a large 14th-century church, of which the main survival is the west façade and its enormous narthex. Looming in the distance, a mirage in the middle of this flat landscape, is a gaunt hill supporting the sinister ruins of the medieval castle of the Counts of Castro, whose fiefdom, the village of Castrojeriz, clings to the arid slopes below.

CASTROJERIZ

Castrojeriz, a village of considerable character, was an Iberian and later a Roman settlement, and during the heyday of the Santiago pilgrimage boasted no less than seven hospitals. The finest of its monuments, the former collegiate church of **Santa María del Manzano**, stands on the eastern outskirts. The church, begun in 1214, but altered in later centuries, retains much of its original transitional Gothic structure, including its west portal, and the arches of its spacious nave; the late Gothic vaulting is of the early 16th century, as is the splendid rose window on the west façade, filled with German stained glass. On the other side of this long, sprawling village is the **Church of San Juan**, the fortress-like tower of which has a Romanesque base; the other parts of the building date from the 14th to 16th centuries and include a partially ruined 14th-century cloister with a fine *artesonado* ceiling.

Castrojeriz: a view of the eastern side showing Santa María del Manzano and the ruined castle above.

TO BOADILLO DEL CAMINO

Medieval village cross at Boadilla del Camino.

The next stretch of the route is over the last hill for many kilometres to come. The view from the top, where a lone cross has been placed, extends over an endless plateau, crossed by a straight and disappearing line marking the route in front of you. Slowly you descend to the Pisuerga river, the tree-lined banks of which make a cheerful and refreshing sight. Standing in a field just in front of the river is a solitary 13th-century chapel, all that remains of the former pilgrims' hospital of San Nicolás. The river itself, spanned by an eleven-arched **Bridge** dating back to the time of Alfonso VI, traditionally marked the frontier of the kingdoms of Castile and Leon; today it represents the border between the provinces of Burgos and Palencia. **Boadilla del Camino**, 9 km (5 miles) west of the river and surrounded by wheat-fields, has a famous **Cross** elaborately decorated with late Gothic ornament and pilgrims' shells.

FRÓMISTA

Frómista: grotesque capital inside church of San Martín.

A more important stop is at the nearby village of Frómista, where you will find one of the purest, earliest and most French of the Romanesque churches of the pilgrims' way. This, the church of **San Martín**, was founded in 1066 by the widow of Sancho the Great of Navarre, and is very reminiscent of a Poitevin hall-church. Its triple-apsed east end — thought by some to be by the same architect as that of Jaca cathedral — is attached to a three-aisled, barrel-vaulted nave; the aisles are virtually the same height as the nave, and thus there is no triforium or clerestory. Transepts extending no further than the aisles flank an octagonal tower recalling that of Irache; the west façade is framed by a pair of bold circular stair turrets. The corbels and capitals throughout the entire building are carved, though many of the capitals, marked with an 'R' in the abacus, are the result of an 1893 restoration and are quite bogus. This drastic late-19th-century restoration, combined with the fact that this church is now a museum and no longer used for services, help largely to explain why the building curiously fails to excite. Its proportions are perfect, the original late 11th-century carvings magnificent, and the geometrical simplicity of its forms highly satisfying; but the whole has the chilly perfection of many a neoclassical building, and little of the warmth normally associated with the Romanesque style.

90

The pilgrims' route from Frómista to Carrión de los Condes follows entirely the asphalted road, a frankly dreary stretch enlivened only by the church of **Santa María** at Villalcázar de Sirga. The village itself, a thriving and important town in Picaud's time, is now a tiny, insignificant place, and its great church strikes an incongruous note. Originally attached to a convent protected by the Templars, it was built in the early 13th century in a tentative Gothic style. On the south side there is an enormously tall porch shielding a richly carved portal, and, above this, two superimposed friezes; in the south transept, below a large rose window, are the fine 13th-century tombs of St Ferdinand's son, Don Felipe (murdered in 1271 by his brother Alfonso X), and of Felipe's wife, Doña Leonor. Opposite the church is a former 16th-century warehouse with a timber-beamed ceiling; it is now an attractive restaurant run by Pablo Payo ('Pablo el Mesonero'), one of the great characters and promoters of the pilgrims' way, and a man who always welcomes pilgrims with free food and wine.

VILLALCÁZAR DE SIRGA

Villalcázar de Sirga: the south side of the former convent church of Santa María.

Carrión de los Condes, described by Picaud as a 'busy and industrious city rich in bread, wine and meat and all kinds of things', has not declined to quite the same extent as Villalcázar

CARRIÓN DE LOS CONDES

and is still a prosperous if not especially beautiful place. The 12th-century church of **Santa María del Camino** on the eastern side of town has a Romanesque south portal with worn and rather crude carvings representing, it is sometimes thought, the legend of the 100 Christian virgins who were given annually to the Moors as tribute money, supposedly on this very spot. An opportunity to study at close quarters the other carvings that decorate the exterior of this quaintly unsophisticated structure is provided to pilgrims who are put up by the parish priest in a makeshift room attached to the building's north side: you will find yourself sleeping directly underneath a row of grotesques sculpted in the corbels. Romanesque carving of a far more advanced kind is to be found in the western side of town, on the west façade of the **Church of Santiago**: there are charming small figures in the archivolt, but the most impressive feature of this façade is the frieze above, dominated by a powerful and intricately carved figure of Christ in Majesty. The pilgrims' route descends from here down to the pleasant banks of the River Carrión, on the other side of which, standing in open countryside, is the great architectural jewel of the town, the Renaissance cloister which is enclosed in what was once the Benedictine monastery of **San Zoilo**. This monastery, later a seminary but recently abandoned save for its porter, dates back to the 12th century: rebuilt in later centuries, it retains from the original Romanesque structure only a small window in the tower attached to the late baroque west façade of the church. The place merits a visit solely for its cloisters, designed by Juan de Badajoz in 1537, but not completed until 1604; late Gothic in form, they are encrusted all over with deeply carved classical decoration, including portrait medallions clinging to pendulant bosses. The whole creates an effect of great plasticity and dynamism, and serves as an excellent introduction to an architect and sculptor whose greatest works are shortly to be seen in León.

Soon after San Zoilo the pilgrims' route once again leaves the road, and creates a straight line across what is one of the flattest and most monotonous stretches of the whole route, an endless expanse of wheatfields in which the occasional clump of trees provides the only landmark. The road is regained once more as you leave Palencia province and head towards Sahagún.

LEÓN
SAHAGÚN TO VILLAFRANCA DEL BIERZO

For most of the province of León, the pilgrims' route continues to make its way across the same desolate plateau which it entered after Burgos. The main difference in the landscape is that the nearer you reach the actual town of León, the more you see of the imposing and often snow-capped mountain-range which rises above the wheat fields to the north and which extends along the whole of Spain's northern coast. In these mountains lies the former kingdom of Asturias, where the Moors halted their advance on the peninsula, and where indeed they suffered, at Covadonga in 722, their first major setback. The Asturian kings, based in Oviedo, soon extended their territory to the south, Alfonso the Catholic even managing by the mid-eighth century to overrun the plains as far south as the Tormes. In around 913 Ordoño II transferred his capital from Oviedo to León, thus bringing into being the

(Opposite) The cloisters of León cathedral which were remodelled by Juan de Badajoz.

(Below) The pilgrims' way from Sahagún to Villafranca del Bierzo.

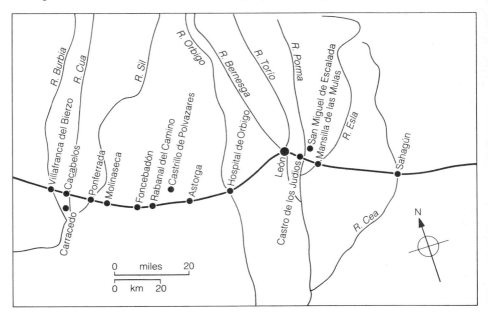

95

large kingdom of León. The power of this kingdom was weakened by the habit of the Leonese kings of dividing their territory among their sons, thus exacerbating relations with Castile and Navarre, and creating a tense, confusing situation from which the Moors profited by making continual forays during the course of the 10th century; in 996 the Moors even recaptured the town of León, and were not to be ousted until six years later. Greater stability ensued with the union of León and Castile in 1037, though, as we have seen, this union was not made definitive until the early 13th century. Even today there are those who appear to resent the joining together of the two regions, and on numerous occasions along the pilgrims' road you will see the word Castilla crossed out from signs promoting the regional government of Castilla y León.

However, the differences in character between the landscape and the architecture of these two regions are slight at first, and it is only to the west of Astorga, when the route climbs into the wild and isolated district of the Maragatos, that you begin to feel truly in some other land. The province of León extends into the adjoining district of the Bierzo, but by now you are in a place far closer in spirit to Galicia than to Castile. The stereotypical Spain of the lonely plateaux is well behind you.

SAHAGÚN

Sahagún, the most important town in between the border of León province and León itself, was referred to by Picaud as 'prosperous Sahagún', a description hardly appropriate to the place of today. A sad and decayed town, Sahagún belongs to a vanishing Spain, with decrepit houses mainly of the early years of this century, and streets and a central square lined — as with so many towns and villages of this region — with blackened, splintering wooden porticoes. In Picaud's day merchants from all over Europe brought vast wealth to the town, as did the presence here of one of the most important Benedictine monasteries in the country. Founded in the ninth century, but twice destroyed by the Moors, this monastery was refounded in the 11th century by Alfonso VI, who submitted it to the Cluniac reform and appointed as its abbot his personal confessor and future Archbishop of Toledo and Primate of Spain, Bernard of Aquitaine. Under Bernard, and aided by vast royal funds, the abbey flourished, so much so that in around 1243 Archbishop Jiménez de Rad, could write that 'As Cluny excels in France, so this monastery stands over all those of its order in Spain.' Attached to this monastery was also a famous pilgrims' hospital, established by Alfonso VI, and functioning up to the end of the 18th century. Then disaster fell, in the form of two fires which destroyed virtually the entire complex, reducing it to an even worse state than Cluny after the French Revolution. Of the monastery there now remains, on the western edge of town, a 17th-century arch absurdly grand for its present surroundings, a tower insensitively transformed into a clock tower, and the adjacent ruins of a 12th-century chapel, the **Chapel of San Mancio**. The latter, despite its piteous condition, is of interest as one of the earliest examples of the Gothic style in Spain, and for having arches constructed in brick, a necessary material in this area devoid of stone, and one which was used in the best known of the town's surviving monuments. Before looking at these, you should pay a brief visit to the neighbouring Benedictine **Convent of Santa Cruz**, which was founded in the 16th century and has a simple whitewashed church with a joyful and overwhelmingly elaborate baroque high altar, a fine example of the Churrigueresque style.

A wooden porticoed street off the main square at Sahagún.

The fame of Sahagún in the history of Spanish architecture is connected with the craftsmen who emigrated here from Islamic Spain, and created out of the local brick pioneering Mudéjar buildings. The earliest such building in Spain is possibly the **Church of San Tirso**, which stands behind the monastery ruins, and dates back to before 1123. It has a tri-apsidal east end emulating in brick the blind arcading to be found in Castillian stone churches of this period; the crossing tower, meanwhile, is comparable to many stone towers of this date, but it is more elaborate, and takes advantage of the greater flexibility of brick to create superimposed arcades of exceptional delicacy. The nearby **Church of San Lorenzo**, to the north of the town's main square, dates probably from the end of the century and has more distinctively Islamic brickwork, as well as blind arches of horseshoe shape. The last and latest of Sahgún's Mudéjar buildings is the **Church of the Peregrina**, which you pass as you leave the town, and which was once attached to a Franciscan monastery and pilgrims' hostel. This desolately sited building, now undergoing much

97

needed restoration, is a rare example of Mudéjar craftsmanship applied to a Gothic structure, and it has also a sacristy featuring the coloured and delightful fragments of Moorish-style stuccowork.

SAN MIGUEL DE ESCALADA

Just outside of Sahagún the pilgrims' route again leaves the road, and for twenty bleak kilometres follows a track running parallel to the León to Palencia railway line; this was always an empty, inhospitable area, and Laffi recounts how he came across the body of a pilgrim being devoured by wolves. Eventually you come to **Mansilla de las Mulas**, a town as poor and run-down as Sahagún, but better preserved and more compact, and with extensive remains of its adobe medieval walls, rising above the river Esla. Today's pilgrims, after crossing the river, go straight to León along the N 601, but in the Middle Ages it seems likely that many of them would have passed the isolated Mozarabic church of **San Miguel de Escalada**. Cut off from the main lines of communication in later centuries, this extraordinary structure could best be reached by boat until comparatively recent times, but now there is a small asphalt road which follows the western banks of the Esla, and goes through several primitive communities where adobe houses can still be seen. The well restored church, in a green but lonely setting at the very end of this road, is the largest Mozarabic church in Spain. Built in the early tenth century by Christians who had immigrated from the Muslim

Exterior of the Mozarabic church of San Miguel de Escalada.

Córdoba, it once formed part of a monastery, the remains of which are a Romanesque tower attached to the eastern end of the church. Running along the whole south side of the building is an elegant portico of horseshoe arches resting on marble capitals carved with delicate acanthus motifs. The interior, now stripped of all later accretions, immediately recalls the Mosque at Córdoba, with its wealth of slender marble columns supporting a variety of different capitals, including ones taken from the Roman site on which the church stands, and others from an earlier Visigothic structure. The main arches of the nave are carried across the chancel to form an *iconostasis*, a reminder that when the church was built the Visigothic rather than Roman rite was celebrated here, a rite which is comparable to that of the Greek and Russian Orthodox Churches today. The *iconostasis* preserves some of its marble panels with bird and floral motifs of Islamic origin, and there is further such decoration in friezes above the screen and around the central apse, a space vaulted in Islamic fashion. The latest part of the church is the ceiling of the nave, a fine *artesonado* ceiling of the Mudéjar period, covered with the coats of arms of León and Castile.

Returning to the N 601 the town of León shortly comes into view, built up between two tributaries of the Esla, surrounded by wheatfields, and set against a distant backcloth of high mountains. A town of Roman origin, its name is a corruption of the Latin *Legio VII Gemina*, a reference to the legion stationed here by the Emperor Galba in AD 70. Though made the capital of a kingdom in 913, its heyday dates from the 11th century, when it was transformed by the Leonese kings into a major political, cultural and spiritual centre, enhanced by the transference here of the bodies of Saints Isidore and Vincent. One of the largest towns in Spain in the 12th century, Picaud wrote of it as being 'blessed with every possible advantage'. 'Dull and decaying' was Richard Ford's assessment of it in 1845, the decline having set in as early as the 13th century, with the definitive union of León with Castile, and the removal of the Spanish court by Peter the Cruel to Seville. Nearby hydro-electric industries, livestock farming and the mining of iron and coal have brought renewed prosperity to León in more

LEÓN

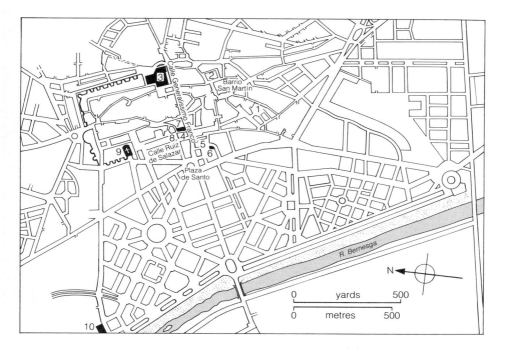

León
1. Plaza del Mercado
2. Plaza Mayor
3. Cathedral
4. Plaza de Botines
5. Plaza de San Marcelo
6. Town Hall
7. Palacio de los Guzmanes
8. Casa Botines
9. San Isidoro el Real
10. Hostal de San Marcos

recent times, and the founding of a university has contributed as well to the new animation.

Though encircled by ever expanding modern development, the old town of León has retained much of its original appearance, even to the extent of having kept most of the defensive walls put up in 1324 by Alfonso XI. The pilgrims' route brings you to the **Plaza del Mercado**, a quiet porticoed square of considerable charm. In between here and the arcaded and somewhat grander 17th-century **Plaza Mayor** extends the **Barrio San Martín**, in many ways the most attractive and medieval-looking part of León, with wooden porticoes, picturesquely askew brickwork houses, and so many bars that the area is generally known as the 'Barrio Húmedo' or 'Humid District'.

LEÓN
CATHEDRAL

From the Plaza Mayor the Calle Mariano D. Berrueta leads directly to the **Cathedral**, one of the great Gothic buildings of Spain. Begun in 1258, it was completed by around 1303 save for the top half of the south transept façade and the south tower (with openwork spire) of the west front, both being executed in the late 15th century by Joosken van Utrecht. The unknown first architect of the cathedral created a daringly high and delicate structure, but was rather too optimistic about the amount of masonry which his buttresses could support. His miscalculation led to numerous problems after the 16th century, beginning with the collapse of the vault in the crossing in 1631; various other architects intervened at later stages, leading to much insensitive and ineffectual restoration, and, in the case of one 19th-century architect, Matías Laviña, almost causing the destruction of half of the building. G.E. Street arrived just after Laviña had got to work, and he

León cathedral
1. Capilla de la Virgen del Camino
2. Museum
3. Cloisters
4. Choir

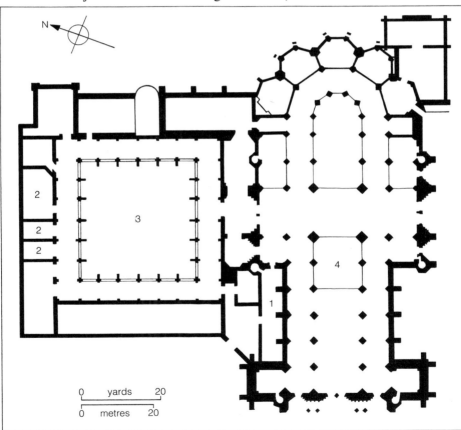

N

| 0 | yards | 20 |
| 0 | metres | 20 |

(Opposite) The west façade of León cathedral.

sincerely wished that he had arrived earlier, so worried was he about this architect's lack of experience: 'in Spain', Street reflected,

> there is absolutely no school for the education of architects, the old national art is very little understood and apparently very little studied, and there are no new churches and no minor churches on which the native architects may try their prentice hands.

Fortunately Laviña died before too much harm could be done to the building, and in the hands of his successors the cathedral was carefully restored back to its original state, while solving the previous structural problems.

León cathedral is easily the most French of Spain's Gothic buildings, and Street went even so far as to say that it was the great exception among Spanish buildings generally and should really be considered as part of French architectural history; for Street this cathedral's very lack of Spanish eccentricities such as are to be found, say, in Burgos cathedral, made it 'one of the noblest of European buildings.' One of the French cathedrals with which it has most in common is that of Rheims, the main difference being that the two towers of the west front are not connected by a curtain wall with the central part of the façade, thus allowing a strange glimpse of buttressing. The west front as a whole is an altogether unsatisfactory structure, redeemed largely by its triple portico, inspired by the transept façades at Chartres. The carvings on the west portals are masterly, as are those on the south and north portals; altogether these sculptures constitute the largest group of 13th-century statuary to be seen in Spain, as well as the main delight of the building's exterior. But it is in the interior that the great beauty of the cathedral is truly felt. Thankfully stripped of all its baroque altars and other accretions, it makes an immediate impact on account of the delicate, uncluttered character and soaring proportions, qualities very uncharacteristic of Spain. Even the choir, though in the centre of the nave as is normal in Spain, does not intrude, its height being small in relation to that of the nave, and its western side being open and taking the form of a classical triumphal arch through which you can see directly down to the High Altar.

The ground-plan of the building is almost identical to that of

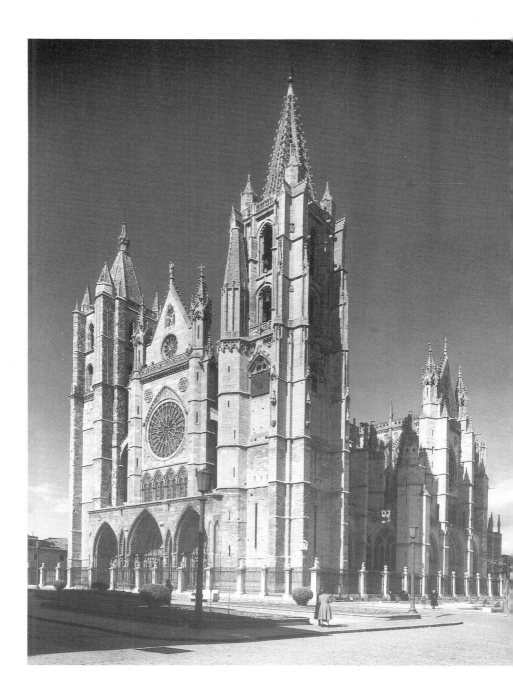

Interior of León
cathedral.

Rheims cathedral, and consists of a three-aisled nave, aisled shallow transepts, and a pentagonal apse with a single ambulatory and five radiating chapels. Two features of French origin which were unprecedented for Spain are the glazed triforium which runs around the whole building, and the way in which the clerestory windows fill all the space in between the slender vaulting shafts. The magnificence of León cathedral is due largely to the fact that the vast amount of window space which the elevation allows is covered all over with stained glass. The windows here constitute together with those at Chartres the finest complex of stained glass to be seen in any medieval cathedral, and are virtually unrivalled in the range of their colouring. Whereas the dominant tones at Chartres and other French Gothic cathedrals are consistently reds and blues, at León these colours vie also with yellows, purples and greens. The windows appear to be exclusively the work of Spanish rather than French artists, and were mainly executed between the 12th and 16th centuries. As for the subject matter this can be divided into three main types: the lower windows of the nave represent trees and flowers common to the León area such as poplars and oaks, the triforium windows feature heraldic motifs, and the clerestory windows are of saints, kings, prophets and so on; these three layers correspond to the natural, human and celestial worlds. Richard Ford suggested that anyone who wished to look more closely at these windows and appreciate their beauty to the full should come here in the evening, when the fading light makes their colours stand out against the darkening mass of the building. Today, on certain nights of the week, another interesting effect can be observed when the interior is brilliantly floodlit and the stained-glass can be seen from outside.

The windows of León cathedral are endlessly absorbing, but the interior does not offer the great range of treasures as is to be found, say, in Burgos cathedral. Of the furnishings special attention should be paid to the choir, which has intricate late 15th-century carvings hidden behind a magnificently elaborate Renaissance exterior designed by Juan de Badajoz. The reconstructed high altar has delicate early 15th-century panels by Nicolás Francés, and there are fine Gothic tombs in the ambulatory and its chapels. Off the north transept, adjacent to a plateresque door leading to the cloisters, is the **Capilla de la**

Virgen del Camino, which was built originally as the cathedral library, and is a spacious late Gothic structure designed by the father of Juan de Badajoz. Juan de Badajoz himself was responsible for the remodelling of the damaged 14th-century cloisters, and gave these — as he did at San Zoilo in Carrión de los Condes — an exuberant covering of classical ornamentation. Off the north side of the cloisters, in a room leading to the Diocesan Museum, is a further example of Badajoz's work, an exquisitely detailed Renaissance staircase reminiscent of a pioneering one by Covarrubias in the Hospital of Santa Cruz in Toledo. In the actual museum, among a host of lesser works, is an outstanding adoration of Christ by the Flemish-born 16th-century artist Pedro de Campaña, and a powerful crucifixion by one of Spain's greatest Renaissance sculptors, Juan de Juni.

West of the cathedral runs the narrow but busy Calle Generalíssimo Franco, at the end of which are the adjoining Plazas de Botines and San Marcelo, which mark the boundary between the old town of León and the new town which grew up from the late 19th century onwards. On the south side of the latter square is the late 16th-century **Town Hall,** an arcaded and elegantly restrained structure by Juan de Rivero. A more imposing Renaissance building of slightly earlier date is the former **Palacio de los Guzmanes** (on the east side of the Plaza Botines), which was probably built by Juan de Rivero to designs supplied in 1559 by Rodrigo de Hontañón, one of Spain's leading architects of this period. More austerely decorated than de Hontañón's celebrated palaces in Salamanca, it features a massive main façade crowned by an upper gallery, and a two-tiered courtyard with depressed arches in the arcades. Adjacent to this palace, on the north side of the same square, is one of the first and the most important of León's late 19th-century buildings, the **Casa Botines** by Gaudi; fringed by the fanciful art nouveau ironwork characteristic of this great Catalan's works, it comprises a rectangular block of rough-hewn masonry flanked at the corners by narrow cylindrical turrets supporting tall pointed spires that seem to come straight from a fairy-tale illustration. West of this building is the Plaza de Santo Domingo, the heart

PLAZAS DE BOTINES AND SAN MARCELO

of the new town, which extends from here down to the river Bernesga. Turning instead to the north, along the Calle Ruiz de Salazar, you will reach the basilica of San Isidoro el Real, a sprawling structure attached to a long section of the town's walls stretching all the way to the cathedral.

SAN ISIDORO EL REAL

The long and complex history of San Isidoro, one of the most important monuments in northern Spain, goes back to a monastery dedicated to St John the Baptist and founded in the mid-ninth century probably on the site of a Roman temple. Rededicated to St Pelayus after this man's relics were transferred to León from Córdoba, it was later destroyed by the Moorish leader Almanzor, and rebuilt in the early 11th century. To the monastery church there was later added a large portico intended to serve as a burial place for the Leonese kings, and this pantheon was to be kept after a further reconstruction of the church in the late 11th century, when the building was rededicated once more, this time to San Isidoro of Seville.

The exterior of the former monastery, as seen from the quiet and charming square on its southern side, is dominated to the left by a tall Romanesque belfry rising over the town's ramparts like a watch-tower. In the very centre of the complex,

The south side of San Isidoro el Real, with the Puerta del Cordero on the left, and the Puerta del Perdón on the right.

crowned by elaborate 18th-century decoration featuring Santiago Matamoros, is a late 11th-century portal known as the
Puerta del Cordero, which has statues of Saints Isidore and
Pelayus flanking its arch, and a tympanum with a lively
representation of the Sacrifice of Isaac. Entering this door you
come to the extraordinary oblong portico built as a royal
pantheon, which has now been separated from the church.
Architecturally this is an exciting and original space, with large
and beautifully carved capitals supporting groined vaulting;
but the place is perhaps best known for its frescoes, which were
added after 1190 and form the finest and best preserved group
of Romanesque frescoes still to be seen *in situ*. From the
pantheon you can walk into the monastery's cloisters, only the
northern side of which is Romanesque, the rest being rather
heavy baroque work. A small staircase near the entrance to the
pantheon climbs up to San Isidoro's excellent museum, which
contains a remarkable group of 11th-century sacred objects,
including the silver reliquary of St Isidore. The obligatory
guided tour of the museum will take you as well into the 16th-
century library, a polychromed and richly stuccoed structure
in pinks and blues, designed by Juan de Badajoz and featuring
such characteristic ornamental motifs of his as pendulant
bosses.

San Isidoro el Real,
Panteón de los Reyes:
(above) a richly
carved capital
supporting the
fescoed ceiling; *(left)*
part of the
Romanesque ceiling
fresco depicting the
Annunciation to the
Shepherds.

To enter the church of San Isidoro you have to return to the square and go through the portal adjoining the Puerta del Cordero; this particular door, attached to the south transept and known as the **Puerta del Perdón**, is also of the 11th century, and has a sculpted tympanum which is unusual for its time in having three scenes grouped together (representing the Descent from the Cross, the Three Marys at the Tomb, and the Ascension). Once inside you will find yourself in a vast barrel-vaulted space built between the late 11th and 12th centuries. Desecrated by French troops in the early 19th century, and subsequently whitewashed and highlighted in brown and white washes, the building was described by Richard Ford in 1845 as 'bedaubed and bepainted in the most barbarous bad taste' and 'only an incongruous shadow of the past'; the overpainting has long since been removed, but even so this heavily restored place has a cold and lugubrious character. The most interesting feature architecturally are the transepts, which extend beyond the lateral apses and open into the nave through vast cusped arches that rise above the clerestory and provide a strong Moorish note. The central apse was the only part of the original Romanesque structure not to survive, being pulled down in 1513 to make way for a late Gothic chancel designed by the father of Juan de Badajoz.

HOSTAL DE
SAN MARCOS

The last but not least of León's important monuments is the former monastery and pilgrims' hospital of San Marcos, which stands next to the river and is reached from San Isidoro by walking due west through the new town. G.E. Street forgot to visit the building, but later regarded the omission as 'a very venial one', knowing as he did that the place was associated with Juan de Badajoz, whose work elsewhere in León had not impressed him (it should be added that he failed, like many people, to distinguish between the son's work and the father's). By leaving out San Marcos, Street had in fact missed one of the supreme masterpieces of the Spanish Renaissance.

Begun in 1514 as a replacement to a monastery and hospital founded in the 12th century, San Marcos received vast funds from Ferdinand the Catholic; work on the building was to be continued right up to the 18th century, though in a style largely in accordance with the Renaissance designs. The original designs were supplied by Don Pedro de Larrea, but carried out at first by Juan de Orozco, who proudly assumed responsibility for the church, the incomplete façade of which bears the inscription *Orozco me fecit*; it was not until 1539 that Juan de Badajoz, together with Martín de Villareal, took over the construction of the complex, Badajoz's main work here being the cloisters and the sacristy. The monastery and hospital continued to function until 1837, after which they were put to the usual miscellany of uses ranging from veterinary school to barracks. Had the civic authorities of León had their way the building would have even been pulled down in 1875. It was at all events in a terrible state of repair by 1961, when its fate was finally secured by being purchased for transformation into a luxury hotel, which now forms part of the Spanish government Parador chain; the church meanwhile continues to function as a church, and should you so want you could even attend mass from the stylish comfort of the hotel.

The cloister of the Hostal de San Marcos, León.

The most celebrated feature of San Marcos is its 100-metre (330 ft) long façade which overlooks the verdant Plaza de San Marcos and on which almost all the decoration of the exterior has been concentrated. The part of the façade which belongs to what is now the hotel is one of the most eloquent expressions of the Spanish plateresque style. The enormously long central block is divided into two levels, the lower of which is articulated by Corinthian pilasters, and the upper one by rather spindly columns hung with swags. Despite the use of columns and swags, there is no significantly greater emphasis given to the upper level than to the lower one, and you certainly do not find here the exaggerated top-heaviness characteristic of so much Spanish architecture. Similarly the frontispiece, though the most elaborate part of the façade and crowned above the balcony by a fanciful baroque pediment thrust up by volutes, does not have quite the same prominence as in other Spanish buildings, where it is usually set against a rather austere background. The façade of San Marcos should perhaps be seen less as an architectural structure than as a magnificent tapestry, covered all over with the full range of classical plateresque ornament, from portrait medallions to candelabra, garlands of fruit to mythological scenes, *putti* to scallop-shells.

Detail from the façade of the Hostal de San Marcos.

The interior of the hotel, entered through an arch

supporting a vigorous representation of Santiago Matamoros, is decorated in the usual mock-medieval Parador style and has little of architectural interest apart from its delightful, shaded cloisters. Comprising a lower storey with tall arches flanked by buttresses, and a smaller and daintier upper storey with depressed arches, these were designed by Juan de Badajoz, but not completed until the 18th century; they are decorated with classical portrait medallions and other plateresque motifs, though in comparison with those on the building's façade these seem quite restrained. A door off the upper storey (if locked ask for the keys at the reception desk downstairs) leads into the upper choir of the church. This is distinguished by some of the most sophisticated and intricate wooden choir stalls to be seen in Spain. The date 1542 and the signature Guillemus Doncel appear under the prior's seat, but it is unlikely that this otherwise unknown artist was responsible for all the work; the dynamism of many of the figures betrays the hand of the great Juan de Juni, who is known to have worked at San Marcos, and was probably the author of some of the more elaborate sculptures in the cloister and on the façade.

After leaving the hotel you should have a more thorough look at the church, the west front of which forms the right-hand corner of the main façade. This front is dominated by a huge porch in the form of a classical arch, the spandrels of which are covered with a profusion of scallop shells. The late Gothic interior has elaborate vaulting, but is otherwise surprisingly simple in its architecture and decoration, the main ornamentation being the scallop shells that cover all the exposed east wall of the chancel, and the spandrels of the raised choir. The real treat of the church is its sacristy, which today houses part of the local archaeological museum (the other part is displayed in a gallery connecting the church with the hotel). The sacristy was wholly the work of Juan de Badajoz, and is perhaps his masterpiece, with its polychromed and complex vaulting adorned with scallop motifs, its shafts resting on corbels in the form of expressive heads, and the overall dynamism and plasticity of its sculpture and ornamentation, culminating in the superlative east wall; where a classical triumphal arch flanked by billowing ornament pushes up the entablature surrounding the room to lift up almost to the ceiling a great pile of deeply carved statuary. With the work of

Badajoz the niceties of the plateresque make way for a style which looks ahead to the baroque. G.E. Street, with his puritanical Victorian biases, would not have liked this development.

The pilgrims' route leaves León by way of the bridge alongside San Marcos, and follows the main road all the way to Astorga. Only 6 km (4 miles) outside the town is a sanctuary housing the much venerated image of the **Virgen del Camino**, the patroness of León. The sanctuary was founded in the 16th century, but the present building dates from the 1950s, and is the work of a monk with the medieval-sounding name of Fray Coello de Portugal. It is by far the most distinguished example of modern architecture along the whole *Camino Francés*, though admittedly this is not saying very much. Taking the form of a rectangular concrete box which has toppled over, its west façade has a great sheet of stained glass of abstract and indifferent designs, produced in the workshops at Chartres. Standing in front of this is a group of bronzed emaciated figures which appear to have been dipped in sulphuric acid; they represent the Pentecost and are well-known works by the Catalan sculptor Subirachs, who can also take the blame for the bronze doors and crucifixes to be seen elsewhere in the church. The interior is largely striking for the contrast between the ugly concrete and the exuberant high baroque altar framing the 16th-century image of the Virgin.

The small town of **Hospital de Orbigo**, 23 km (14 miles) further on, has a famous long bridge of Roman origin, spanning a mossy tree-lined stretch of river. But the next place of major architectural interest is Astorga, which rises up on a small hill and is still surrounded by its old walls, which date back to Roman times. It was once the capital of a small county, but was joined to León in the 13th century, and has been a place of minor importance since then; its sleepy old-fashioned character will appeal to those with a hankering for traditional Spain. On the main square, which you pass shortly after entering the town, is an outstanding 17th-century **Town Hall** with a façade comprising a tall frontispiece crowned by an elaborate belfry

Detail of the baroque
main portal of
Astorga cathedral,
showing *columnas
ajarronadas.*

and joined by flying buttresses to flanking twin towers. The arrangement of this façade recalls that of Astorga's cathedral, which in turn seems to have been inspired by that of León's. The present **Cathedral** was begun in the late 15th century to designs supplied possibly by Juan Gil de Hontañón, whose son Rodrigo certainly took over some time the following century; work was continued in the baroque period, and was not complete until the very end of the 18th century, when the neo-classical sacristy was built. Unquestionably the most exciting feature of the building is the baroque frontispiece on the west front, a towering structure of extraordinary ornamental complexity rising above a portal encrusted all over with intricate statuary; a typical feature of the baroque of this region — and a feature which was to be transposed successfully to Latin America — are the so-called *columnas ajarronadas*, columns with shafts ringed by superimposed bands of acanthus and other bulbous ornamentation. The late Gothic interior in greyish-green stone has a dusty, lifeless look, and is largely of interest for its Renaisance high altar, the masterpiece of Gaspar Becerra, an Andalusian artist who learnt his craft in Italy. Off the decaying classical cloisters is an appropriately gloomy and badly arranged Diocesan Museum.

Adjoining the cathedral is the **Bishop's Palace**, Astorga's most popular monument and the major work by Antonio Gaudí outside his native Catalonia. The strange presence in this backward conservative town of a building by one of the great avant-garde architects of turn-of the-century Europe is due entirely to the remarkable Bishop of Astorga, Juan Bautista Grau y Vallespinós. A fellow Catalan and a good friend of the fervently Catholic Gaudí, Grau commissioned the building from Gaudí partly out of a spirit of Catalan nationalism, but largely as a way of stimulating the economic and cultural life of his then impoverished diocese. The choice of architect aroused enormous local hostility, which the charismatic and visionary Grau did his utmost to placate. Sadly, however, he died in 1893, only five years after the first stone had been laid. The continuing controversy, combined with long delays in receiving payment, proved too much for Gaudí to deal with on his own, and he eventually abandoned the work, resolving never to set foot in Astorga again. Work on the building was taken up again in January 1894, but it was not until the 1960s that it was finally to be completed. The building, in its overall conception, is no less fantastical than Gaudí's Catalan buildings, but the master's failure to supervise most of the construction work is clearly evident in the generally lack-lustre detail. The exterior, with its picturesquely asymmetric arrangement of turrets, buttresses and 'witch-hat' spires, resembles a futuristic fairy-tale castle, but it has none of the polychroming, range of materials, and innovative iron-work that characterize Gaudí's finest Catalan work. The slightly faded interior, housing an uninteresting museum of the Santiago pilgrimage, and an even worse collection of local contemporary art, has a basement of brick vaults and an insipid series of ground-floor rooms with columns highlighted in pale, institutional brown. But a visit here is made worth-while by the tall and spacious main floor, which is seen to its best advantage on a sunny day, when the colours from the stained glass are projected on the walls and floor, thus enhancing the architect's mysterious use of space. You have the feeling of wandering through some enchanted forest as you walk from the darkened chapel to the rooms that open up around it, each completely different in detail and colouring.

The Bishop's Palace, Astorga, designed by Antonio Gaudí.

BEYOND
ASTORGA

Along the top of Astorga's western ramparts runs a popular promenade looking out towards an imposing range of mountains, the Montes de León, the highest peaks of which, snow-capped for much of the year, receive the first rays of the morning sun. Ahead of you extends the wildest and one of the most beautiful stretches of the pilgrims' way, which from here leaves the N 160 and follows a narrow minor road along which only the occasional car passes. The handful of villages that you go through as you cross the mountains have been largely abandoned, though many of their attractive houses have recently been bought as holiday and week-end homes. This is the land of the Maragatos, an ethnic group of much disputed origin, who led an isolated existence over the centuries and who preserved until very recently a strong folk culture. The village of **Castrillo de los Polvazares**, only 6 km (4 miles) from Astorga and just off the pilgrims' route, is famous for its folk architecture. Today an over-prettified show-piece, it has cobbled streets lined with solidly built stone houses from which project the occasional wooden balcony. **Rabanal del Camino**, an important stop on the pilgrims' way and once protected by the Templars, has similarly picturesque buildings, but is in an evocative state of decay; the tiny church of Romanesque origin has a rustic interior of toy-like charm and a rather more robust belfry of later date, from which excellent views can be had down to the distant plains of Astorga. After Rabanal the landscape becomes ever more mountainous and spectacular as you climb up to the pass of **Foncebadón**, which is marked by a tall iron cross buttressed by heavy pieces of slate thrown by generations of passing peasants and pilgrims. You descend steeply into the narrow and densely fertile valley of the Bierzo, a valley speckled in the spring months with the white blossom of thousands of cherry trees. To the medieval pilgrim, the Bierzo was an ante-chamber to Galicia, a foretaste of the great natural riches that according to Picaud lay in store for them in that region. For today's traveller, however, all bucolic and celestial thoughts are dispelled on arrival at the Bierzo capital of Ponferrada, a mining town which immediately calls to mind the industrial communities of South Wales or Pennsylvania.

PONFERRADA

The remains of Ponferrada's old town stand above the eastern banks of the river Sil, and include a large **Templar Castle** built in the late 12th century, enlarged in the 14th century, and in apparently perfect condition until vandalized by the French in 1811; with its turrets and fantastical machiolations it is still an amusing place to visit, though it has been so restored that it seems more like a papier-mâché model than a real building. The town's main church is the nearby **Santuario de Nuestra Señora de la Encina**, which contains yet another miraculous image of the Virgin, this one discovered by the Templars in 1200, hidden in the holm oak tree or *encina* which gives the building its name. A 16th-century structure with baroque additions, it has a single-aisled late Gothic interior with fanciful vaulting in the crossing. From here the pilgrims' route follows the attractive Calle del Reloj, passing underneath a 16th-century gate crowned by a baroque clock tower; on the much rebuilt main square beyond this is an impressive 17th-century Town Hall, an austerer version of the one at Astorga.

Ponferrada: the Templar Castle.

Before crossing the Sil, you could make a brief detour to see the church of **Santo Tomás de las Ollas**, which occupies a hilltop position on the eastern outskirts of town, off the main road to Madrid. Dating back to the 11th century, and as such the oldest surviving church in the Bierzo, it has a Mozarabic apse ringed with blind arcading of horseshoe shape.

The part of Ponferrada which is built on the western banks of the Sil is completely modern and dominated by a great slag-heap. Even the most determined pilgrim would be best advised to take a bus from here to the town of Cacabelos, 12 km (7 miles) away, and thus avoid a dull and heavily developed stretch of the Bierzo valley. Cacabelos itself is of little interest, but a fascinating detour can be made from here to the former Benedictine **Monastery of Carracedo**, 3 km (2 miles) to the south, in an agreeable green and wooded setting. The monastery was founded in 990 by Bermudo II 'the Gouty', whose father, Ordoño III of León, had a summer residence here; but it was not until the early 12th century, under the rule of the Abbot St Florentine, that it became a place of major importance, receiving enormous funds and support from Alfonso VII and his sister Doña Sancha. In the late 18th century a vast neoclassical church was begun in replacement of an earlier Romanesque structure built by Alfonso VII in around 1138. However, work on the new building had not been completed by the time the French arrived in 1811 and forced the monks to flee; extensive remains of the original structure can still be seen in the west end of the church, including a large rose window and a tower. The rest of the monastery, unoccupied since the early 19th century, is in ruins, and at present undergoing heavy restoration. Well-preserved parts of the old complex can none the less be seen on the eastern side of the destroyed Gothic cloisters, most notably a late Romanesque chapter house containing carved capitals, and the remains of the tiny royal palace built by Alfonso IX in the early 13th century; the so-called 'Queen's kitchen' has tall and elegant columns supporting Gothic arches, while the 'Queen's Balcony' outside eloquently illustrates the transition between the Romanesque and Gothic styles, with arches and windows fringed by delicate beading.

CARRACEDO

VILLAFRANCA DEL BIERZO

Villafranca del Bierzo, at the western end of the Bierzo, huddled between two fast-flowing rivers and the verdant foothills of the Galician mountains, is one of the most beautiful small towns of northern Spain. Described by Ford as 'truly Swiss-like', Villafranca is very different in its architecture to other Castillian towns, having slate grey houses fronted with large and glazed projecting balconies such as you will find in Galicia. G.E. Street, like Ford before him, was taken by the picturesqueness of the place, but failed to find here any monuments that betrayed the town's important past. Clearly he had not seen the Romanesque **Church of Santiago**, which stands above the town, and is the first building you come to as you catch the first glimpse of Villafranca from the pilgrims' way. This, after following the N VI all the way from Cacabelos, deviates on to an attractive path 2 km (1 mile) before Villafranca, and takes you alongside the northern flank of the Santiago church. This single-apsed building is simple in its architecture and decoration, almost all its carvings being concentrated on the impressive north portal, which is known as the Puerta del Perdón, for it was here that all the pilgrims who felt unable to continue their journey west would receive all the absolutions that they would have done at Compostela itself. The heavily worn carvings are all on the capitals and arches of the door, and include scenes of the Epiphany and the Crucifixion, and a powerful Christ in Majesty in the keystone. The rather bare interior of the church features at the west end a crude Romanesque baptismal font adorned with shell motifs.

(Above) Villafranca del Bierzo: exterior of the apse of the Church of Santiago.

(Below) The Puerta del Perdón, Church of Santiago.

After passing next to the town's well-preserved late 15th-century castle, the pilgrims' way descends down the narrow **Calle del Agua**, the town's finest street and lined on both sides with imposing 16th- and 17th-century palaces, the austerity of which is partially compensated for by a series of large and flamboyantly carved coats of arms. The route crosses the fast-flowing Burbia before heading off in the direction of Galicia, but there are other interesting buildings still to be seen in the town. On a hill-top position adjoining the Santiago church is the **Church of San Francisco**, originally part of a Franciscan monastery founded in the 13th century. The church has a transitional Romanesque portal on its much restored west façade, and a late Gothic east end; but its most outstanding feature is the enormous *artesonado* ceiling in the nave, constructed in the 14th century, but painted in the middle of the following century. Just to the north of San Francisco, off the town's oval main square, is the massive **Jesuit College**, a baroque structure with a façade partially inspired by that of the Jesuiti in Rome, and featuring an upper storey composed of two large flanking consoles and a broken pediment of Michelangelesque derivation; the bare grandeur of the interior is paralleled in many churches of the Galician baroque. The most interesting church in town is the incomplete **Collegiate Church of Santa María of Cluny**, in a small parkland setting by the River Burbia. Attached once to a Cluniac foundation, as its name suggests, it had fallen into ruins by the 14th century, and was completely reconstructed from the early 16th century onwards; work was continued up into the 18th century, but then abandoned, leaving the west end unfinished. The great Rodrigo Gil de Hontañón was responsible for the main design of the building, which, like other works of his, is remarkable for its blending of Gothic and Renaissance elements. Especially impressive are the vast proportions of the interior, which includes transepts with late Gothic vaulting and a crossing enclosed by huge round piers decorated with Renaissance motifs.

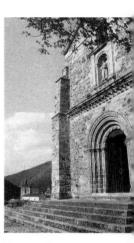

The west façade of San Francisco.

West of Villafranca the pilgrims' route follows for a while the busy La Coruña road, climbing slowly up the narrow Valcarce valley, and passing through a series of pretty, old-fashioned villages, where Galician is the principal language spoken. At Herrerías you turn on to a footpath and begin the steepest and also most spectacularly beautiful section of the whole *Camino Francés*, with vast panoramas extending down to the distant Bierzo valley. Beyond the remote hamlet of Laguna de Castilla, well above the tree-line, and along a path which can have changed little since medieval times, you reach a stone marking the boundary with Galicia.

GALICIA
CEBREIRO TO SANTIAGO DE COMPOSTELA

Aymeric Picaud, evoking the landscape which extends west from the mountain of Cebreiro, conjured up images of a promised land. Galicia was for him a place

> abundant in woods, delightful for its rivers, meadows and exceptionally rich orchards, its wonderful fruit and clearest of streams . . . it abounds in rye bread and cider, cattle and horses, milk and honey and all sorts of seafood; it is rich in silver and gold, textiles and furs, and, above all, in Saracen treasures.

The fact that Galicia marked the end of the pilgrims' journey undoubtedly contributed to Picaud's idealized picture, as did the similarities that he found between it and his native France. For him the Galicians, 'above all the other uncultured races of Spain', were those 'closest to our French race in their customs.'

Anyone travelling to Galicia will certainly become immediately aware of how radically different the region is to other parts of Spain, its character being far closer to northern than to southern Europe. The people, in comparison to most other Spaniards, can be sullen and unwelcoming, and are suspicious at first of foreigners. The wooded, rain-washed landscape, hilly and mountainous, is coloured a predominant grey and green, and forms a complete contrast to the arid plateaux of Castile. The parts of Europe that are unfailingly compared with Galicia are those with a strong Celtic legacy such as Ireland, Cornwall, and Brittany. The Celts indeed came to Galicia in the sixth century BC, and their influence is felt in the bagpipes, granite crosses, and folk legends of this highly superstitious region. The Romans came next, and, after them, a Germanic tribe called the Suavians, who in AD 409, turned Galicia into an independent kingdom. Overrun by the Visigoths in the following century, and later briefly occupied by the Moors, Galicia was finally incorporated into the kingdom of the Asturias. Though it had lost its independent status at a very early stage in its history, the region has been rather

(Opposite) Casas y Nóvoa's baroque masterpiece — the Obradoiro façade of Santiago cathedral.

119

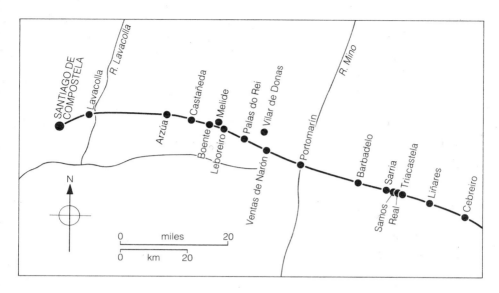

The pilgrims' way from Cebreiro to Santiago de Compostela.

isolated over the centuries from the rest of the country, and is much closer in its language, customs and folklore to Portugal than to Spain. Despite the pilgrims' route to Santiago, communications between Galicia and elsewhere in Spain have generally been poor, and only recently has road travel within the region been significantly improved. It is a region which has been notorious for its poverty and backwardness, a situation which has resulted in large-scale emigration. Scarcely industrialized in the last century, it also has a terrain which is largely unsuitable for cultivation, and which has suffered too from the unprofitable system of *minifundios*, or small-scale farming. The landscape is parcelled into tiny plots of sloping land, each divided from the other by granite slabs in the earth, and defended by ferocious dogs that provide present-day pilgrims with their greatest hazard.

The very backwardness of Galicia has led to the persistence here of a strong folk culture. For those following the pilgrims' route through the region, one of the main features of interest are the many old-fashioned rural communities which you pass, places where wooden clogs are still widely worn and where fascinating examples of folk architecture can be seen, beginning with the extraordinary *pallozas* at Cebreiro. The rural architecture is generally of slate and granite, and one of the ubiquitous and attractive features of the farms here are the *horreos*, or tiny barns that are raised above the ground on mushroom-like pillars of granite and are decorated with crosses that give them the appearance of strange funerary monuments. The architecture of the towns meanwhile is notable for its glazed projecting balconies (often extending up several floors), a fashion originating in the seaside town of La Coruña and intended to maximize on the little sun which the region receives, while protecting from its frequent winds. As for churches, the main styles are the Romanesque and the baroque, both of which here have a somewhat sombre character owing to the heavy grey stone usually employed by the architects. The baroque buildings of Galicia, though disgracefully ignored by most visitors, are among the most original of this region's architectural achievements. The sobriety of the planning and of the materials generally used is

belied by a remarkable ornamental inventiveness, as for instance in the works of Casas y Nóvoa, who was responsible both for the celebrated Obradoiro façade of Santiago cathedral, and for much of the nearby monastery of San Martín Pinario. More unusual still is the rigidly geometrical decoration evolved by other baroque architects in Santiago, and inspired probably by the working methods of marquetry workers. This bizarre style, so suited to the hardness of granite, is a telling reflection of a land so idiosyncratic and full of fantasy.

The pilgrims' way on the last stages of the climb to Cebreiro: the view looking back towards the Bierzo.

CEBREIRO

Cebreiro, the exposed mountain-top hamlet to which you come almost immediately after crossing the Galician border, is an appropriate place to begin a tour of this region. Shrouded in legend, it is identified by many with the Breton tale of Walfran, and is thought also to be the place to where the Holy Grail was brought by pilgrims, the nearby castle of Balboa being the fortress of the Parsifal hero Klingsor. The inhabitants of the place, reduced now to a handful of people living in rough-hewn stone dwellings, have traditionally survived off the growing of rye and potatoes, and the tending of flocks. Originally they all lived in *pallozas*, circular dwellings of probably Celtic origin, a group of which can be seen on the western slopes of the hamlet. Covered by large, conical straw roofs, they feature low walls that are made up of stone or granite, and are generally windowless on account of the freezing winds of the area. In plan they comprise two semicircular segments of unequal size separated inside by a large dividing wall; within the two segments humans and farm animals would live in close proximity. One or two of the *pallozas* in the vicinity are still inhabited, but of those in Cebreiro itself, two now function as a tiny ethnography museum, and another serves as a particularly cold and damp pilgrims' hostel.

Traditionally the pilgrims that passed through Cebreiro would be put up at the hostelry attached to the small Benedictine monastery founded probably in the ninth century. The monastery's decline had set in by the end of the 16th century, and its church and hostelry were in a piteous state when rescued in the early 1960s by Father Elías Valiña, a priest who devoted much of his life to researching the Santiago pilgrimage. The simple slate hostelry is now a tiny hotel, endearingly homely and unpretentious, and far more traditional in character than are those buildings given a mock medieval chic by the Spanish Parador chain. The adjacent **Church**, also in slate, has probably kept much of its ninth-century plan, if virtually nothing of the original masonry. The undecorated three-aisled interior with rectangular apse and wooden beam ceiling, is whitewashed save for its arches and columns. Displayed in a glass-fronted safe in the right aisle are a chalice and reliquary relating to a miracle which once enjoyed international fame: at a mass celebrated here in around 1300, the host and communion wine turned literally into flesh and blood, thus confounding the rather. cynical officiating priest, and rewarding the sole person in the congregation, a peasant who had braved a terrifying winter storm to come here. The chalice is a wonderful example of 12th-century Romanesque goldsmith work, while the reliquary was a gift of Ferdinand and Isabel, who came here as pilgrims in 1486.

Soon after Cebreiro, begins a gradual and beautiful descent into a landscape ever more studded with farms, hamlets and tiny plots of land. There are no more mountains to climb, but the terrain between here and Santiago remains constantly hilly, and there are difficult muddy paths to negotiate, and numerous dogs to appease. Between the small town of **Triacastela** — where there is a rustic church of Romanesque origin — and the larger community of **Sarria**, you can either walk across country along the original pilgrims' route, or else take the LV 634, which follows the attractively wooded Ouribio valley, and passes next to the important Benedictine monastery of Samos. Pilgrims have frequently left the *Camino Francés* to visit the latter, where the monks continue to this day to offer great hospitality to those travelling to Santiago. Before reaching the monastery, you skirt the well-preserved village of **Real**, where the low and irregularly-shaped stone houses, with their large, low-pitched slate roofs, blend perfectly into the contours of the landscape.

SAMOS

The **Monastery of Samos** itself, in a bucolic wooded setting by the banks of the Ouribio, dates back to the sixth century, and as such is one of the oldest Benedictine foundations in Spain. Abandoned after the coming of the Moors in the early eighth century, it was shortly afterwards rebuilt, and there survives today, a hundred metres from the present monastery, a delightfully rustic slate chapel of the late ninth and early tenth centuries, with a rectangular apse (as at Cebreiro) and a toy-like appearance enhanced by an old and massive cypress tree which towers above its southern flank. The present monastery, erected between the 11th and 12th centuries, was rebuilt following a fire in the early 16th century, and then

Samos: the west
façade, designed by
Juan Vázquez, of the
monastery church.

extended in the 17th and 18th centuries; a further fire in 1951
led to extensive renovation and reconstruction. The complex
features two cloisters, the smaller of which retains one of its
original Romanesque doors, but is otherwise in a late Gothic
style. The larger cloister, dating from the end of the 17th
century, represents Spanish architecture of the baroque period
at its most austere, and is distantly indebted to the uncompromising classicism of Juan de Herrera; the inner walls on the
upper level are relieved by some hideous contemporary
paintings of the life of St Benedict, while in the centre is a
modern statue to the Enlightenment reformer Feijóo, who was
a monk here in the early 18th century. It was Feijóo who
encouraged the construction of the present, enormous monastic church, and moreover helped towards its costs with the
money received from some of his publications. The church,
built between 1734 and 1738 by the Samos monk Juan
Vázquez, has an interior almost as severe as the large cloister
to which it is attached. This barrel-vaulted interior, with a
restrained high altar by the well-known Galician sculptor J.
Ferreiro, is in fact reminiscent of that of the monastery church
of El Escorial, but without the dazzling colour provided in the
latter by the vault frescoes of Luca Giordano; the main note of
colour at Samos is that of the polychromed figures of
Benedictine saints adorning the squinches of the crossing. The
west façade of the church, though by the same architect, is in
a different style to the interior, and is indeed the most

genuinely baroque feature of the whole complex. Though incomplete and missing the upper part of its towers and a crowning pediment, it still manages to convey a sense of drama and movement through the contrast between wide flanking piers and twinned central columns, through the use of deeply incised ornament, and, above all, through the incorporation of a complex double-ramp staircase of a type probably inspired by that of the Obradoiro of Santiago cathedral.

SARRIA

Sarria, an important centre in medieval times, is today a large and thriving market town with extensive modern development. The remains of medieval Sarria are to be found in a quiet outlying district at the top of the town, and include the modest Romanesque **Church of the Salvador**, the ruins of a **Castle**, and the former hospital and monastery of **La Magdalena**. The latter, now a monastery of the Mercedario order and still functioning as a pilgrims' hostel, is a 13th-century foundation which has been entirely restored and altered in later years; its main interest is its 14th- to 15th-century church, which has flamboyant Gothic features of the Isabelline period. From Sarria onwards the pilgrims' route runs parallel to the C 533, and goes through increasingly muddy terrain. There is little of architectural interest, apart from the isolated Romanesque **Church of Santiago de Barbadelo**, the finest feature of which are the worn carvings on the simple west portal; the single aisle interior with its wooden beam ceiling is in a rustically decayed state and has kept few of its Romanesque elements.

PORTOMARÍN

Ten kilometres (6 miles) further on, from the top of a wooded hill, you look down over the pretty Belesar reservoir across to the modern village of Portomarín. The construction of the reservoir led to the old village being submerged under water, but the best of its buildings were transferred to the new settlement, a rather strange place arranged alongside a long, porticoed main street resembling a film set. The most important of these buildings is the large Romanesque parish **Church of San Juan**, a curious fortress-like structure comprising a single rounded apse attached to a tall and crenellated rectangular block which has a rose window on its western side, and blind arcading on the two flanking ones; these three sides have richly carved late 12th-century portals, the authorship of which was once attributed to the celebrated Master Mateo, the sculptor responsible for the Pórtico de la Gloria of Santiago cathedral. When the church was transferred to its present site, its baroque high altar and other later additions were removed (much to the indignation of the villagers) and the whole stripped down to its original Romanesque simplicity; the end result is that the unusually wide single-aisled interior, elegant though it is, has a cold and slightly inhuman look, in fact rather like the new village itself.

VILAR DE DONAS

A far more moving Romanesque building than San Juan is the former monastery church of **San Salvador** at Vilar de Donas, situated in a quiet rural setting 15 km (9 miles) to the west of Portomarín, and 2.5 km (1½ miles) to the north of the pilgrims' route. The monastery, founded at the end of the 12th century, was attached to the Order of Santiago, several of whose knights lie buried in the church. The church, built in the first half of the 13th century, is an interesting example of the survival in Galicia of Romanesque forms alongside Gothic ones; here the remains of a Cistercian Gothic portico are adjacent to an exuberantly ornamental Romanesque portal. The tall and single-aisled interior, stained by damp and evocative dark green, has a narrow Romanesque arch separating the nave from the crossing and proportionately small transepts. The rounded central apse, the same height as the crossing, is covered on its lower level with some of the most important surviving frescoes from 15th-century Galicia; among the paintings are heads of the prophets Jeremiah and Daniel, and scenes of the Resurrection and the Annunciation, the latter in a remarkably good condition considering the obvious humidity in the church. Of the medieval furnishings, special mention should be made of the beautifully carved late 15th-century stone *baldacchino* in the north transept: this liturgical canopy is a form quite common to Galicia.

San Salvador de Vilar de Donas: the west façade showing the Cistercian Gothic portico.

MELIDE

For its last 80 km (50 miles) the pilgrims' route runs parallel to the busy C 547, the towns and villages along which are largely of no great beauty or architectural merit. Of these places, the sprawling town of Melide has perhaps the most to see, having a much restored Romanesque church with a decorative west portal (**San Pedro**), and the delightful **Plaza del Convento**, which is surrounded by old buildings, including the former monastery **Church of Sancti Spiritus** (now the Parish Church), which has a baroque exterior, and a Gothic chancel. On the western outskirts of Melide the pilgrims' route passes through the hamlet of **Santa María**, where there is a decayed Romanesque church containing interesting 12th-century carvings as well as a series of frescoes of about the same date as those at Vilar de Donas. The immediate approach to Santiago is today particularly unappealing, following as it does the main road into the town from Santiago airport; a route where pilgrims risk being killed on the last stage of their journey. The airport is named after the river Lavacolla (the name of which is derived probably from the Latin for 'arse-wipe'), where pilgrims traditionally cleaned themselves prior to arrival at the promised city. Their first glimpse of Santiago would be from the hill called Monte del Gozo, which today rises desolately above the Autopista del Atlántico.

Today a ludicrous modern statue of a pilgrim with outstretched arms marks one of the entrances to Santiago itself. After such an unpromising start, however, you are soon confronted by what is unquestionably one of the most beautiful and intact of Spain's old cities. Traditionally pilgrims would make their way to the cathedral along what is now the Rúa de San Pedro, entering the formerly walled town by the gate which once stood on the square named today the Puerta del Camino: from here they would head west past the small triangular-shaped Plaza Cervantes (the site of the old Town Hall), and arrive eventually at the Plaza Azabachería, in front of the cathedral's north transept. The town, like the cathedral itself, is built on uneven ground, and its largely traffic-free centre is made up of a warren of narrow, granite-paved streets that seem constantly to ascend and descend. G.E. Street, though so full of enthusiasm for the cathedral, found the rest of the town to be a 'disappointing place', his disappointment stemming from the fact that the granite buildings that lined its

SANTIAGO DE COMPOSTELA

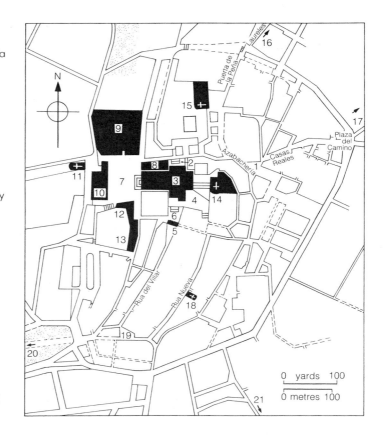

picturesque streets were mainly of 17th- and 18th-century appearance. Although Santiago is generally thought of as a medieval town, its medieval elements — including even the cathedral — are cloaked by what must be one of the most extensive ensembles of baroque architecture in Europe. Another feature of Santiago, and to many tourists its most depressing one, is its perpetually wet climate, a climate which according to Ford earnt the town a reputation as '*El orinal de España*'. Ford described Santiago as 'damp, cold and gloomy-looking', but to many of the town's enthusiasts it is precisely these qualities that give the place its peculiar charm, which is so wonderfully evoked in the lyrical, wistful works of the popular turn-of-the century poetess Rosalía de Castro. Certainly the rain has softened the granite look of the town, blurring the harsh contours, tinting the grey with a greenish fur, and encouraging the growth of lush vegetation in its cracks and crevices. Furthermore the melancholy aspects of **Santiago** are more than compensated for by an underlying vitality, which owes much to the town's university and to its myriad of bars famed for their astonishing range of sea-food. At the very centre of Santiago's life, and dominating every vista, is the cathedral, from the many doors of which scurry forth a continual succession of clerics who, like the priests in some Spanish 19th-century novel, prey on all the local gossip. The massive variegated bulk of the building, almost a town in its own right, sits at the convergence-point of Santiago's network of streets, its tutelar's tomb acting, in the powerful words of Ford, as 'a spider in the middle of its web, catching strange and foolish flies'.

The whole history of Santiago begins with its cathedral, for beforehand the town was of but little importance. The original cathedral was begun shortly after Bishop Theodomir of Iria Flavia discovered here in 813 the body of St James. The first building, commissioned by Alfonso II, soon proved inadequate for the growing number of pilgrims, and a second structure was put up on the orders of Alfonso III and consecrated in 899. In 997 Moorish hordes razed this and the rest of the city to the ground, leaving only the tomb of St James, which — according even to Islamic sources — they were too afraid to touch; the large bronze bells of the cathedral were taken to Córdoba, but they were to be returned here in the 13th century, and can now be found in the middle of the cloisters. It was not until 1075 that construction of the present building was begun, promoted by Bishop Diego Peláez, who, however, was to be deposed as bishop in 1081, accused of complicity in a plot to invite William of Normandy to Spain. By the end of the century the bishopric of north-western Spain was to be transferred from Iria Flavia to Santiago, and soon afterwards came to be upgraded to archbishopric. The first archbishop was the dynamic Diego Gelmírez, one of the great political and cultural figures of his age, and whose forty-year rule at Santiago (he died in around 1140) is generally regarded as a golden age in the history of the town and its pilgrimage. Gelmírez brought most of the great Romanesque cathedral to completion by 1128, and commissioned as well cloisters and a

The towers of the Obradoiro façade seen from the cloister; their Romanesque bases can be clearly seen.

large palace to be built respectively on the southern and northern sides of the building. Another intensive building campaign began in 1168 led to the embellishment of the west front with Master Mateo's celebrated Pórtico de la Gloria.

Numerous modifications were made to the cathedral over the following centuries, and work was even started in the 13th century on a projected Gothic reconstruction. The cloisters were rebuilt in the 16th century, which also saw the foundation of Santiago's university, and the city's conversion into the official capital of Galicia. During the 17th and early 18th centuries the vast accumulated wealth of the cathedral authorities resulted in the building's exterior being almost entirely shielded by baroque work, culminating in Casas y Nóvoa's spectacular Obradoiro. The town itself, however, began losing its importance in the 18th century, and its decline was to be hastened after being temporarily succeeded as Galician capital by La Coruña. Whereas the latter developed into a thriving modern city, Santiago stagnated, and its centre has been little changed over the last 100 years.

SANTIAGO
CATHEDRAL

A tour of Santiago has to begin with its cathedral, the different façades of which all overlook some enchanting square. The **Plaza de la Azabachería**, the former meeting-place for all those who had travelled along the *Camino Francés*, had in Picaud's day an ornate fountain of Paradise with a basin large enough to accommodate an estimated 15 pilgrims, who would cleanse themselves here before entering the cathedral through the door of the north transept. In between the fountain and the door was a small market where scallop-shells and other souvenirs would be sold; surrounding the square itself were the workshops of the many craftsmen who specialized in *azabache* or jet jewelry. The original north door, described at length by Picaud, was known as the Door of France, and had a central column representing Christ in Majesty and flanking scenes of Adam and Eve and the Expulsion from Paradise. Sadly the whole façade of the north transept was pulled down in the late 18th century to make way for the least satisfactory of the cathedral's later additions, an unhappy compromise between the baroque and neoclassical styles begun in 1750 according to plans by Ferro Caveiro y de Mariño and completed by a

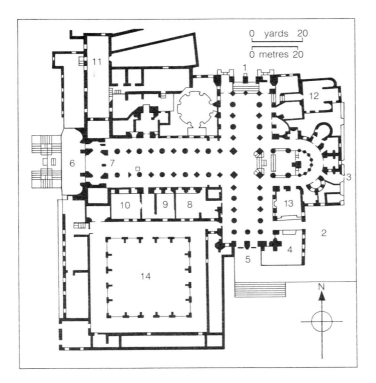

0 yards 20

0 metres 20

Santiago cathedral
1. Puerta de la Azbachería
2. Plaza de la Quintana
3. Puerta Santa
4. Torre de la Trinidad
5. Puerta de las Platerías
6. Obradoiro façade
7. Pórtico de la Gloira
8. Sacristy
9. Treasury
10. Reliquary chapel
11. Palacio Gelmírez
12. Capilla de la Corticela
13. Capilla del Pilar
14. Cloister

N

Galician follower of Ventura Rodríguez. As for the square itself, this too was transformed in the 18th century, when it lost its fountain and market atmosphere, and acquired the imposing main façade of the Monastery of San Martín Pinario.

Walking from here around the cathedral in a clockwise direction, the next square which you come to is the **Plaza de la Quintana**, which is known also as the **Plaza de los Literarios** in memory of a student battalion formed at the time of the Peninsular War. The square, built on two levels joined by a great flight of steps, faces the south side of the cathedral's apse, which is encased by late 17th-century walls crowned by balustrades and elaborate finials. The famous **Puerta Santa**, opened only during Holy Years (years in which St James' day, 25 July, falls on a Sunday), comprises a stiff and mannered 17th-century framework bizarrely incorporating in its sides 24 Romanesque figures largely taken from the cathedral's destroyed Romanesque choir (the lower figures are modern

The Puerta Santa.

imitations). The most dramatic baroque addition to this side of
the cathedral is unquestionably the Clock Tower or **Torre de la
Trinidad**, which towers over both this square and the adjacent
Plaza de Platerías. Completed in the early 18th century by
Domingo de Andrade, its top half consists of an extraordinary
range of architectural and ornamental forms piled up in
tapering fashion to an enormous height.

The Plaza de Platerías, the smallest of the squares surrounding the cathedral, is lined on two sides by loggias where silver-
workers have traditionally shown their wares. The south side
of the square is framed by the impressive 18th-century **Dean's
House**, which is decorated in the strange geometrical manner
characteristic of the so-called Compostelan baroque. Rising

above steps on the opposite side of the square is the façade of the cathedral's south transept, the most extensive surviving part of the original Romanesque exterior. The twin-arched south portal, probably the first door to be executed in the cathedral, has tympana tightly packed with carvings of the Life of Christ, the sculptor of which has been identified with that of the south door of the new church of San Isidoro in León; the expressive elongated figures in the reveals recall instead those in the cloister of Moissac in the Dordogne. Above the arches are grouped a crowded miscellany of further Romanesque figures, some taken from other parts of the cathedral, including from the destroyed Door of France. On the upper level are two arched openings, richly ornamented and with a central polylobed arch which suggests that the architect was either Spanish or else deeply immersed in Spanish culture.

Finally comes the enormous **Plaza de España** or **del Obradoiro**, which provides a suitably spacious and monumental foreground to what is one of the most exciting west façades of any Spanish cathedral, and one of the most famous achievements of the Spanish baroque. Part of the drama is provided by its double-ramp staircase, which was built in the late 17th century and is the oldest part of the façade: inspired possibly by the Golden Staircase in Burgos cathedral, which in turn was derived from Bramante's Belvedere staircase, it is more complex than either of these two works, rising as it does on three rather than two flights of steps. The rest of the façade, executed at remarkable speed between 1738 and 1750, was the work of Casas y Nóvoa, who incorporated into his design the twin towers from the Romanesque building. Above the disguised Romanesque towers, with their decorative Lombard bands, soar tapering piles of ornament comparable to that of the Clock Tower, but with an obsessive use of volutes which brings to mind Longhena's Santa Maria della Salute in Venice. The volute motif is freely used in the even more elaborate frontispiece, which is shaped at the top more like the elongated gable of a Flemish house than the pediment of a church. What gives this structure its unmistakeably Spanish quality is its chaotic and richly carved profusion of sculpture and ornament.

G.E. Street, coming to Santiago in 1863, did not know what to expect of the cathedral, and half believed that all he would find would be 'the mere wreck of an old church, overlaid everywhere with additions by architects of the Berruguetesque or Churrigueresque schools'. When he found instead, behind all the later accretions, an outstandingly well preserved Romanesque building, he was quite amazed, as are indeed many first-time visitors to the cathedral today. You only have to go through the door at the foot of the great flight of steps on the Obradoiro façade to be transported back 600 years. Behind the door is a crypt which was once thought to be an earlier cathedral, and is still referred to as the '*Catedral Vieja*'. Built in fact by Master Mateo in the late 12th century as a support for the Pórtico de la Gloria above, it features tranverse arches, the bosses of two of which have representations of angels holding the sun and the moon. Quite probably the whole iconographic programme of the Romanesque cathedral was intended to reinforce the idea of the building as a representation of the celestial Jerusalem, the vault of the crypt symbolizing the celestial vault on which the heavenly group of the Glory rests.

Up to as late as the 16th century, Santiago cathedral remained open throughout the day and night, the massive triple-arched **Pórtico de la Gloria** being a doorless structure which once opened out directly on to the square. Scandalous activity resulting from pilgrims sleeping in the cathedral led to the portal being enclosed by outer doors, and since that time the view has been impeded of Master Mateo's sculptural masterpiece, which is signed by him on the lintel of the central arch, and bears the date 1188. Among the wealth of figures portrayed on the tympanum are Christ and the Evangelists, while on the archivolt above are the 24 elders of the Apocalypse, most of whom bear musical instruments depicted so realistically that they have provided enormous assistance to musicologists. On the jambs are free-standing figures of the apostles, and around the right-hand arch are representations of heaven and hell; there are countless other scenes and details, not all of which have been convincingly explained, for instance the jamb-figures of the left-hand arch. St James dressed as a pilgrim is seated in front of the central pillar, and you can see at his feet the indentation left by millions of pilgrims putting their hands there as a gesture of thanksgiving for their safe arrival at Santiago; on the other side of the pillar is a kneeling figure popularly thought to represent Master Mateo himself,

Master Mateo's masterpiece: the Pórtico de la Gloria.

and on whose head believers traditionally rest their own to draw inspiration from that great mind. The whole portal has echoes of the great Cluniac one at Vézelay, but Master Mateo is generally claimed as Spanish, and all his authenticated work is in Galicia. At all events the realism and liveliness of this sculptural ensemble, in which the whole Heavenly Host appears to be on the point of breaking out into song, make it one of the most eloquent expressions of Romanesque art, and its life-like and magical qualities must once have been enhanced by the polychroming which covered it; traces of polychroming remain, but these are from a 17th-century restoration campaign.

The figures of St Peter, St Paul, St James the Less, and St John, on the central portal of the Pórtico de la Gloria.

The first impression on passing through the Pórtico de la Gloria into the brown granite interior is of exceptional unity, and you cannot help but agreeing with Picaud's assessment of the place:

> In this church there is no fault; it is admirably constructed, large, spacious, light, with harmonious dimensions, well proportioned as to length, width and height; it is more splendid than words can express. It is even built on two floors, like a royal palace.

Above the tall and elegantly proportioned aisle arches, arranged into single bays by columns supporting the ribs of the central barrel vault, runs a gallery comprising arches with rounded tympana and slender paired shafts. Unlike in other pilgrimage churches, where it stops short at the chevet, the gallery at Santiago runs around the whole building. Covered with quadrant vaults, it is big enough to hold a large congregation, though today is officially closed to the public. Should you be lucky enough to have permission to climb up to the gallery, the beauty of the cathedral is more apparent than ever, as Picaud himself suggested:

> Anyone who walks around the upper parts and who started off unhappy would leave happy and contented after having contemplated the perfect beauty of this church.

Much of the initial impact of the cathedral's interior is due to the uninterrupted view down to the chevet, the cathedral being one of the few in Spain not to have its choir at the east end of the nave. This has not always been the case, for,

The nave of Santiago Cathedral looking towards the baroque high altar.

ironically, Santiago had been apparently the first Spanish cathedral to promote the fashion for placing a walled choir in so obstructive a position, the innovation having occurred during the rule of Diego Gelmírez. The Romanesque choir, one of the few stone ones in Spain, was destroyed in the 17th century (fragments can be seen in the cathedral's museum) and replaced by a baroque one which in turn was removed earlier this century. The removal of the choir encouraged excavations in the nave that led to the discovery of foundations of the pre-Romanesque cathedral and of an ancient burial ground which included the tomb of Bishop Theodomir; with special permission you can go underneath the nave to visit these finds.

A great shaft of light directs your way down the nave to the crossing, where you will find a 14th-century lantern remodelled during the baroque period. Suspended underneath this like a giant spider is a metal frame from which the baroque silver censer known as the *Botafumeiro* is swung on special occasions, a spectacle of unforgettable power. The revolutionary mechanism employed dates back to the Middle Ages, and as you watch mesmerized and terrified as the censer swings in a cloud of smoke backwards and forwards the whole length and height of the wide transepts, you can rest assured that it has fallen off only twice during its long history.

Off the east end of the northern transept is the Romanesque **Capilla de la Corticela**, really a church in its own right which was incorporated into the fabric of the cathedral. It is a tri-apsidal, three-aisled structure supporting a wooden ceiling, and preceded by a 13th-century tympanum of the Adoration of the Magi, Christianity's first pilgrims. As you walk from the transept into the ambulatory, with its radiating chapels, you near the goal of the pilgrimage — the relics of St James. These are kept in a silver coffer underneath the High Altar, and are reached by way of a narrow marble crypt of the late 19th century. Emerging from the crypt up into the southern side of the ambulatory, pilgrims return to the northern side by climbing into the high altar itself, where they kiss the robe attached to a 13th-century image of St James. As with the wide transepts, the altar is so planned that a continual stream of tourists can pass through it without interrupting the cathedral's liturgical functions. The exuberantly baroque altar in gilded wood — hiding eight columns from the Romanesque cathedral — is not the most sophisticated of the building's baroque additions, its outsized angels supporting the crowning canopy being perhaps more appropriate to a fairground than to a cathedral. More sophisticated baroque work is to be found in the sumptuous 18th-century **Capilla del Pilar**, situated at the junction of the ambulatory and the south transept, and built to designs supplied by both Domingo de Andrade and Casas y Nóvoa.

A plateresque door off the west side of the south transept leads you into the 16th-century **Cloisters**, the work of several architects, including two of the leading figures associated with 16th-century Salamanca, Juan de Alava and Rodrigo Gil de Hontañón. Whereas the exterior of the cloisters is in a wholly Renaissance style, the interior comprises Gothic arcading and intricate late Gothic vaults. A characteristically plateresque feature is the elaborately worked crowning balustrade; more unusual are the stepped pyramidical corner towers that suggest Aztec influence, a not wholly implausible source of inspiration given the New World interests of many of Santiago's archbishops at that time. Among the rooms lying off the cloister are an archive containing the *Codex Calixtinus*, and a museum with a lugubrious basement featuring tantalizing fragments of Master Mateo's original Romanesque cloister. In the upper rooms of the museum are a series of tapestries after Goya, and an outer gallery with excellent views of the Plaza del Obradoiro. Further treasures of the cathedral, including medieval reliquaries and late Gothic silverwork by members of the Arce family, are displayed in the chapels off the south side of the nave.

The cathedral at Santiago acts as such a powerful draw for tourists that the town's numerous other buildings of interest are often neglected. A great many of these buildings are its immediate surroundings, a particularly fine series — spanning six centuries — being those that line the Plaza del Obradoiro. The **Palacio Gelmírez**, on the south side of the cathedral, is the oldest, having been constructed as an archbishop's residence between the 12th and 13th centuries. Within are two outstanding halls, the lower of the two having two lines of groin vaulting supported on tall piers of great slenderness and

OTHER
BUILDINGS IN
SANTIAGO

elegance; the upper hall, originally used as a dining-room, has vaulting sprung from corbels carved with scenes appropriate to the room, such as plates, goblets and musicians. Adjacent to the palace is the imposing **Pilgrims' Hospital** commissioned by Ferdinand and Isabel, and largely built by Enrique Egas between 1501 and 1509; it functioned as a hospital up to 1953, when it was transformed into a luxury hotel in the Parador chain. As with other palaces of the plateresque period, the ornamentation of its long façade is concentrated mainly on its retable-shaped frontispiece, which is Renaissance in detail but Gothic in plan, and with a row of crowning pinnacles which is quite medieval in character. Typical also of the plateresque is the wide and ornate entablature which runs along the top of the façade and combines egg-and-dart moulding with a naturalistic chain motif. The remaining masonry is relieved of its austerity by two long balconies resting on fantastical consoles, a baroque embellishment but one which is wholly plateresque in spirit, and comparable to work by Rodrigo Gil de Hontañón in Salamanca. Inside the former Hospital are four courtyards (two of which are of the baroque period) centred around a 16th-century chapel now used for exhibitions and receptions; the finest part of the chapel is the crossing, which is separated from the nave by a Renaissance grille, and is decorated at the corners by piers covered with overwhelmingly intricate Gothic statuary and ornamentation.

In the angle in between the Hospital and the adjacent **Palacio de Raxoy** is a balcony overlooking the **Church of La Angustia de Abajo**: designed in 1757 by Lucas Ferro Caaveiro, its western façade is a good example of the geometrical Compostellan baroque, with deeply carved volutes, and giant order piers articulated by projecting square plaques. The enormous Palacio Raxoy, which takes up the whole western side of the square, is only slightly later in date than Ferro Caaveiro's church but could hardly be more different in style, being an unmistakeably French building of the neoclassical period, and in fact the work of the French architect Charles Lemaur; designed originally as a seminary, it is now the Town Hall. Framing the southern side of the square is the **Palacio de San Jerónimo**, which was built in the 16th century as a University college, and is now the seat of the Rectorate. A great curiosity is its portal, a 15th-century work taken from a demolished pilgrims' hospital and in a style which could be described either as staggeringly backward or, more favourably, as Romanesque revival. The palace is joined today to the 16th-century **Palacio de Fonseca**, which has an elegant courtyard and a lecture hall with a fine *artesonado* ceiling.

On the **Plaza de la Quintana** is the **Convent of San Pelayo de Antealtares**, originally a Benedictine monastery founded by Alfonso II at about the same time as the cathedral; the present structure dates from the late 17th and early 18th centuries, and contains in its church a magnificently gilded and polychromed baroque high altar. Impressive though this altar is it palls in comparison with the baroque delights that await you in the nearby church attached to the former monastery of

The 16th-century west façade of the former monastery church of San Martín Pinario.

San Martín Pinario. This enormous complex deserves to be the major sight in Santiago after the cathedral, though in fact it is one of the most neglected, being little known even to the people of the town. Founded apparently by the early tenth century, it too once belonged to the Benedictines, whose role in the early history of Santiago was of key importance, theirs being the first religious order to be entrusted with the protection of the apostle's tomb. The present complex dates from after the 15th century, when the three main Benedictine foundations in the town decided to come together. The monastery façade, overlooking the Plaza Azabachería, is a majestic if rather austerely decorated work of the early 18th century. Its frontispiece, begun by Gabriel Casas, comprises a

San Martín Pinario
1. Monastery façade
2. Claustro de la Porteria
3. Claustro de las Oficinas
4. Staircase
5. Church façade
6. Baroque staircase
7. High altar
8. Choir
9. Sacristy
10. Capilla del Socorro

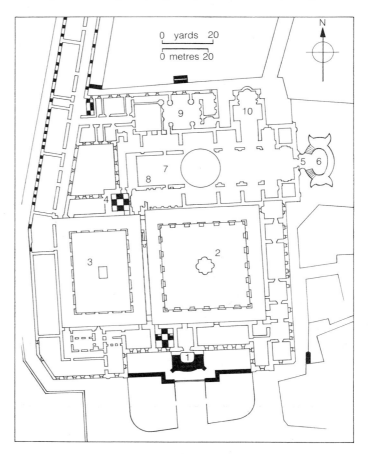

giant order of paired columns rising above a flight of steps and supporting an elaborate crowning piece designed by Casas' great pupil, Fernando Casas y Nóvoa. Beyond this portal you come to the **Claustro de la Portería,** an enormous cloister begun in 1633 but brought to completion by Casas y Nóvoa, who articulated it with further pairs of giant columns and might also have been responsible for the fountain in the middle. Off the adjoining **Claustro de las Oficinas** is a staircase of 1681 with an elaborately carved dome and a fanciful balustrade bizarrely featuring pre-Columbian motifs, a reflection perhaps of the monks' missionary activities.

The monastery has also a fascinating old pharmacy, and a small museum. But its highpoint is without doubt its **Church,** which was begun at the end of the 16th century and turned over a century later into one of the great repositories of the Spanish baroque. Its late 16th-century façade on the Plaza San Martín — directly in front of a building supposedly intended as a Museum of the Santiago Pilgrimage — is the work of the Portuguese architect Mateo López, and features a stiff, retable-style frontispiece divided into three symbolical layers. More interesting than the actual façade is the 18th-century staircase which leads up to it, a complex and ingenious oval construction which coils down and then up again, and has no other purpose than to provide a most dramatic approach to the church: designed by the Dominican monk Manuel de los Mártires, it is perhaps the most excitingly baroque of all Santiago's many fine 18th-century staircases, and is unlike any other staircase in Spain, being comparable only to works in Sicily and southern Italy. The vast, barrel-vaulted interior of the church, built mainly in the course of the 17th century, is simple in plan and has a geometrical elegance and austerity, the fanciful embellishments to the masonry being limited largely to the corbels supporting the monks' gallery. Such an impressively restrained architecture powerfully sets off the dazzlingly intricate early 18th-century furnishings, most notably the high altar by Casas y Nóvoa, a work described by Ford as being 'of vilest churrigueresque . . . a fricassee of gilt gingerbread'. Whatever your tastes in architecture, however, it would be difficult to suppress astonishment in front of this extraordinary altar, a gilded, polychromed structure so overcharged with swirling ornament that it defies rational analysis, and from which rise up, as if from some monstrous dream, the triumphant equestrian figures of St Millán and St James the Moor-Slayer, ejecting as they do so the anguished bodies of defeated infidels. Beyond this free-standing, action-packed altar lies the **Choir**, resting under a coffered barrel-vault highlighted in reds, blues and greens, and adorned with early 17th-century choir-stalls of virtuoso elaboration and detail. Much still remains to be seen in the church, including various Bernini-inspired altarpieces by the great Ferreiro (one of which ingeniously conceals a door). Above all you must visit the **Sacristy and the Capilla del Socorro** (the second chapel to the right in the nave), both of which were designed by Casas y Nóvoa. The former is in the shape of a Greek Cross, and shows the architect at his most harmonious and subdued, the main drama being provided by the powerfully carved figures that ascend on billowing clouds above the entablature. The chapel meanwhile represents the architect at his colourful, ornamental best, and is dominated by another breath-taking gilt altar which doubtless would have been derided by Ford.

The works of Casas y Nóvoa might be the most sophisticated baroque creations in Santiago, but they are by no means the most bizarre or original. The latter honour must surely be held by the frontispiece to the **Convent of Santa Clara**, which is in the north-eastern corner of town, a ten minute walk from San Martín along the Puerta de la Peña and its continuation, Laureles. Designed by Simón Rodriguez in the mid-18th century, it marks the apotheosis of the Compostelan geometrical style, and brings the Spanish love of top-heaviness to its almost ludicrous conclusion. Above the small portal abstract ornamentation of increasing size and protrusion is precariously piled up until eventually a massive cylinder is reached, perched in gravity-defying fashion on top of a structure which could almost be mistaken for some fantastical work of the present century. Near this convent (the interior of which is disappointingly ordinary) is the former **Monastery of Santo Domingo**, a largely baroque complex but shielding a delightful 14th-century church, a rare example of the Gothic style in Santiago. The monastery itself has been turned into the ethnographical **Museo del Pueblo Gallego**, which is worth a visit if only for the unusual double spiral staircase by Domingo de Andrade, a baroque work of magical elegance.

The Convent of Santa Clara: the frontispiece designed by Simón Rodriguez.

South of the cathedral runs the porticoed **Rua del Villar**, the narrow but lively main street through the old town, its many smart shops jumbled picturesquely together. Similarly attractive is the parallel **Rua Nueva**, on which stands the diminutive church of **Santa María**, with its 14th-century Gothic portico protecting a Romanesque portal; inside, on the left, is a baroque altar with the curious feature of tiny sculpted angels wearing spectacles. Both streets will take you to the **Plaza del Toral**, where a statue of Atlas carrying an enormous globe crowns an 18th-century palace built for the Marquises of Bendaña. From here it is a short walk to the west to the **Alameda**, a evocative turn-of-the-century park popular with evening strollers, and with a hill-top position commanding a much-photographed view of the cathedral: it was from this very hill that Ford himself drew the cathedral, its baroque features suitably blurred by distance.

Interior of Santa María del Sar.

For anyone beginning to tire of the baroque architecture of Santiago, it might come as a relief to visit the 12th-century Romanesque church of **Santa María del Sar**, which rises above fields on the south-eastern outskirts of town. This isolated tri-apsidal structure, pinned down on its lateral sides by large buttresses, has frequently been likened to the helm of a ship. The buttresses were put up in the 18th century, and as soon as you enter the church you immediately understand why they were necessary. The interior, with its main apse ringed by superimposed rows of blind acading, would under normal circumstances have immediately impressed through its elegant simplicity. But your attention is diverted instead by the tall nave arches that directly support the barrel vault. Serious subsidence has led to these splaying outwards in dramatic if also rather quaint fashion, giving the impression that the architect was heavily under the influence of the excellent local wines. To regain your own balance you should go outside into the restful cloisters, where one of the Romanesque wings survives, richly covered with ornament, possibly from the hand of Master Mateo.

NOTES FOR FURTHER READING

The literature on the Santiago pilgrimage is vast and ever expanding. Of the recent scholarly works on the subject, the fullest is unquestionably the Council of Europe exhibition catalogue, *Santiago de Compostela, 1000 ans de Pèlerinage Européen*, Ghent, 1985: it has essays by different authors on every conceivable aspect of the pilgrimage, and contains a bibliography of over 450 publications. Other important general works include Bottineau, J., *Les chemins de Saint-Jacques*, Paris, 1983 (1st edition, 1964); Goicoechea Arrondo, E., *Rutas Jacobeas*, Estella, 1971; King, G., *The Road of St James*, (3 vols), New York, 1920; and Vázquez de Parga, L., Lacarra, J.M., and Uría Ríu, J., *Las Peregrinaciones a Santiago de Compostela*, 3 vols., Madrid, 1949 (reprinted Oviedo, 1981). Two good short introductions in English are, Hell, V. and H., *The Great Pilgrimage of the Middle Ages*, London, 1966, and Brian and Marcus Tate, *The Pilgrim Route to Santiago*, Oxford, 1987. The best summary of the various legends of St James is Kendrick, T., *St James in Spain*, London, 1960. The social and psychological history of medieval pilgrimages is admirably dealt with in Davies, H. and M.-H., *Holy Days and Holidays: the Medieval Pilgrimage to Santiago*, London, 1982, and Sumption, J., *Pilgrimage: an Image of Medieval Religion*, London, 1975; a more recent work is Nolan, M.L. and S., *Christian Pilgrimages in Modern Western Europe*, University of North Carolina Press, 1989. Most of the modern accounts of the journey to Santiago tend to be amateurish and tediously sentimental. Two exceptions are Mullins, E., *The Pilgrimage to Santiago*, London, 1974, and the eccentric Irish writer Walter Starkie's characteristically entertaining and fantastical, *The Road to Santiago*, London, 1951. Those wishing to cycle to Santiago might be interested in Neillands, R., *The Road to Compostela*, London, 1985. Horse-lovers should read Hanbury-Tenison, R., *Spanish Pilgrimage*, London 1990.

No recent guide-book to Spain has ever equalled in wit and comprehensiveness Richard Ford's *Handbook for Travellers in Spain*, 3 vols., London, 1845 (most recent edition, London, 1966); the most useful available guide in a practical format is Robertson, I., *Blue Guide Spain*, London, 1989. The regional government of Navarre publishes remark-

ably cheap booklets on most of the important towns and monuments in this region in the extensive series, *Navarra, Temas de Cultura Popular*. Excellent and detailed guides to Burgos, León, and various other towns and districts along the pilgrims' way are produced by the new León publishers, Ediciones Lancia; glossier in format but wider in its coverage of places, are the many local guides brought out by Ediciones Everest, including, José Carro Otero, *Santiago de Compostela*, 1987. The famous 12th-century pilgrims' guide included in the *Codex Calixtinus* exists in a parallel Latin–French edition edited by Vielliard, J. (Paris, 1984); this guide has recently been translated into Spanish by Brazo Lozano, M. (*Guía del Peregrino Medieval*, Sahgún, 1989), while a condensed English version is to be found in the Appendix of Layton, T.A., *The Way of St. James*, London, 1976. The main modern guides to the pilgrims' way are *Guía de Peregrino: el Camino de Santiago*, Madrid, 1985, Bernès, G., *Le Chemin de St Jacques en Espagne*, Paris, 1986, and *Guías Anaya: El Camino de Santiago*, Barcelona, 1990.

The only detailed general account in English of Spanish architecture is Bernard Bevan's useful but very dated, *History of Spanish Architecture*, London, 1938. For Romanesque architecture see Conant, K.T., *Carolingian and Romanesque Architecture, 800–1200*, Harmondsworth, 1966; Gudiól Ricart, J., *Arquitectura y Escultura Románica*, Ars Hispaniae V, Madrid, 1948; and Whitehill, W.M., *Spanish Romanesque Architecture of the 11th century*, Oxford, 1941 (reprinted 1968). Among the more specialist studies are Cayetano Enriquez de Salamanca, *Jaca y el romanico*, León, 1983; and Esteban Lorente, J.F. (and others), *El nacimiento del arte rómanico en Aragón, Arquitectura*, Zaragoza, 1982. An introduction to the Romanesque generally in Spain is M. Gómez-Moreno's classic *El Arte románico español*, Madrid, 1934; the indispensable work on sculpture of this period is A.K. Porter's exhaustive *Romanesque Sculpture of the Pilgrimage Roads*, Boston, 1923; the most recent work on this subject is Marcel Durliat's beautifully produced *La Sculpture Romane de la Route de Saint-Jacques: de Conques à Compostelle*, Mont-de-Marsan 1990. To be looked at if only for their beautiful black and white photographs are the books on the Romanesque art and architecture of the Spanish regions published in the series *Zodiaque, La nuit des temps*, St. Léger Vauban (the ones featuring the monuments on the pilgrims' way are, *Aragon Roman*, 1971, *Castille Roman [vol. 1]Galice Roman*, 1973, *Leon Roman*, 1972, and *Navarre Romane*, 1967; all have summaries in English). Traditional accounts in English on Spanish architecture of the Gothic period include Harvey, J., *The Cathedrals of Spain*, London, 1957, and Street, G.E., *Some Account of Gothic Architecture in Spain*, London, 1869; the subject is dealt with more fully in Torres Balbas, L., *Arquitectura Gótica*, Ars Hispaniae, vol. VII, Madrid, 1952. The pioneering work in English on the plateresque is Prentice, A., *Renaissance Architecture and Ornament in Spain*, London, 1893 (new edition with introduction by Harold W. Booton, London, 1970); the main works in Spanish are Camon Aznar, J., *La arquitectura plateresca*, 2 vols., Madrid, 1945, and Chueca

Goitia, F., *Arquitectura del siglo XVI*, Ars Hispaniae X, Madrid, 1953. For the baroque period see the short summary in Blunt, A. (ed.), *Baroque and Rococo Architecture*, London, 1978; Kubler, G., *Arquitectura de los siglos XVII y XVIII* Ars Hispaniae, Madrid, 1957 is the standard history in Spanish. The principal studies of the Galician baroque are Chamos Lamas, M., *La arquitectura barroca en Galicia*, Madrid, 1955, and Bonnet Correa, A., *La arquitectura en Galicia durante el siglo xvii*, Madrid, 1966.

Useful addresses

Confraternity of St James, 57 Leopold Road, London N2 85G

Los Amigos del Camino de Santiago, Apartado 20, Estella, Navarra, Spain

Peregrino. Boletino del Camino de Santiago, Apartado 60, 26520, Santo Domingo de la Calzada, La Rioja, Spain

GLOSSARY

artesonado: elaborate wooden coffered ceiling imitative of leather work.

baldacchino: canopy above throne, altar or doorway.

chevet: east end of a church.

Churrigueresque: profusely ornamental late baroque style named after the Churrigueras, who were in fact among the least 'Churrigueresque' of Spain's baroque architects.

clerestory: upper stage of the main walls of a church above the aisle roofs, pierced by windows.

crocket/crotchet: carved decorative feature projecting from spires, gables, canopies and other Gothic forms.

crossing: space at intersection of nave, transepts and chancel of church.

depressed arch: low arch in shape of basket and often referred to as 'basket arch'.

iconostasis: screen in Byzantine churches separating the sanctuary from the nave.

Mozarabic: name given to churches, etc., built by Christians living under Islamic rule.

Mudéjar: Muslims working for Christian masters; the name given to their architectural style.

narthex: covered and enclosed space in front of main entrance to church.

plateresque: term applied to Spanish buildings of late 15th and 16th centuries with intricate ornamentation imitative of the work of *plateros* or silversmiths; a distinction is often made between the 'Gothic' or 'Isabelline' plateresque (late 15th-century) and the classical plateresque (16th-century).

spandrel: triangular space between arch and entablature.

squinch: arch constructed across the corner of a square space to make the transition to a dome.

triforium: arcaded wall-passage facing on to nave, and situated above arcade and below clerestory windows (if there are any).

tympanum: area between the lintel of a door and the arch above it.

volute: a spiral scroll as on Ionic column.

voussoir: one of the bricks or wedge-shaped stones forming an arch.

CHRONOLOGY

ACKNOWLEDGEMENTS

Author's acknowledgements

The research for this book has been extremely enjoyable, above all for the enormous amount of help, hospitality and friendship which I have received in Spain. Scholarly assistance was provided by Pedro de Manuel of the Generalitat de Catalunya; Francisco de Beruete, founder and president of Los Amigos del Camino de Santiago at Estella; Don José Maria Díaz, canon and archivist at Santiago cathedral; and the director and staff of the Museo Nacional de las Peregrinaciones at Santiago. Nacho Cabano and Manolo Silva both looked after me wonderfully at Santiago, and shared with me their great knowledge of the pilgrimage. There are three people in particular whom I want to thank in Spain, all of whom accompanied me for part of my journey along the pilgrims' road. Javier Landa, director of the excellent Hotel Candanchú at Candanchú, entertained me in the Pyrenees and went with me from there to his native village of Dicastillo, near Estella. Annie Bennett kept up flagging spirits during the long walk across the daunting Castillian plateau, and braved with me the dogs and wilds of the Maragatos. Matilde Mateo Sevilla joined me on the last stage of the walk, acted as an outstanding guide around her native Galicia, and freely shared her specialist expertise on 19th-century attitudes towards her great namesake, Master Mateo; she also kindly read through a copy of the manuscript.

The writing of this book was begun in the Luberon home of John and Christiane O'Keeffe, who will probably never want to hear the word 'Santiago' mentioned ever again; Jackie Rae provided her usual support, encouragement and companionship. Finally I must thank Marion Marples of the Confraternity of St James, my agent, Mic Cheetham, the photographer Colin Dixon and the friendly and efficient staff at Johnson Editions, in particular my editor Louisa McDonnell and the picture researcher Emma Milne.

Photographs

The publishers would particularly like to thank Colin Dixon for the special photography he undertook for this book.

The author: pp. 3, 6, 20, 32, 39, 47, 57, 59 (right), 87, 90 (top), 97, 109, 114, 124; Colin Dixon: cover photograph, pp. vi, 10, 12, 14, 22, 23, 24, 26, 28, 29, 31, 40, 42, 44, 49, 53, 54, 58, 59 (left), 63, 64, 66, 70, 71, 72, 78, 84, 88, 89, 90 (bottom), 91, 93, 94, 98, 104, 106, 107, 112, 113, 116, 117, 118, 121, 126, 132, 134, 136, 139, 142, 143; A.F. Kersting: pp. 80, 86, 103, 129, 135; Lauros-Giraudon: p. 7; Mary Evans Picture Library: p. 8; Museo Lázaro Galdiano, Madrid: p. 2; Royal Institute of British Architects: pp. 5, 13.

INDEX